THE ENNEAGRAM FOR CHRISTIAN COUPLES

THE ENNEAGRAM FOR CHRISTIAN COUPLES

A Guide to Understanding Your Personality
Types and Deepening Your Relationship

DANI COOPER

ROCKRIDGE
PRESS

Interior and Cover Designer: John Calmeyer
Graphic Designer: Jarod Denmark
Art Producer: Hannah Dickerson
Editor: John Makowski
Production Editor: Holland Baker
Production Manager: Jose Olivera

Illustrations © 2021 Jacinta Kay, cover and pp. X, 22, 96.
Background textures used under license from Creative Market.
Author photo courtesy of Vandy Visuals.

Paperback ISBN: 978-1-63878-600-9
eBook ISBN: 978-1-63878-323-7
R0

To Shane,
my biggest blessing
and greatest supporter.

None of this
is possible
without you.

I love you
with all I am.

CONTENTS

Introduction ix

PART I

The Enneagram 1

PART 2

The Enneagram for
Understanding
YOURSELF
23

PART 3

The Enneagram for
Understanding
YOUR PARTNER
97

I THE PERFECTIONIST	25	
2 THE HELPER	33	
3 THE ACHIEVER	41	
4 THE INDIVIDUALIST	49	
5 THE OBSERVER	57	
6 THE LOYALIST	65	
7 THE ENTHUSIAST	73	
8 THE PROTECTOR	81	
9 THE PEACEMAKER	89	

I THE PERFECTIONIST	99
2 THE HELPER	105
3 THE ACHIEVER	111
4 THE INDIVIDUALIST	117
5 THE OBSERVER	123
6 THE LOYALIST	129
7 THE ENTHUSIAST	135
8 THE PROTECTOR	141
9 THE PEACEMAKER	147

Closing
153

Resources and
References
154

Index
156

INTRODUCTION

Hi! I'm Dani. I'm a mom and wife, music lover, nature addict, and certified Enneagram coach. Previously, I spent 17 years as the worship leader of our church, working with people from many different cultures and backgrounds, seeing God's beauty in the different expressions of each person. I think getting to know and love so many different types of individuals has fueled my passion for learning what makes people tick, and I'm convinced we can make this world a better place by leaning into each other instead of pulling away.

Learning that I'm a Type One on the Enneagram gave me so much new insight into myself, and further study of the system helped me see the people around me in new ways, too. The Enneagram's funny name simply means "nine-drawing," which refers to the related geometric figure that maps "lenses" through which each of nine personality types sees the world. The Enneagram helps us identify the lens we ourselves see through while also teaching us about the eight other (different but equally valid) lenses through which others see. So many relationship problems result from misunderstandings, simply because we all experience the events of life so differently.

Because of the insight the Enneagram provides into the core fears and desires that we and others have, the Enneagram is a powerful tool for cultivating compassion for the ways we all struggle, and I have faith that everyone can benefit from the insight and freedom that God offers us through it. It's important to me that you approach this introduction to the Enneagram with the understanding that you are unique and have been created in love to be in relationships with others. In fact, our collective belovedness is the foundation I want to build this book upon. Understanding that we and the people in our lives are beloved will help us know how God sees us and inform and transform how we relate to and love one another.

If you're ready to deepen your connection with yourself and those with whom you are in a relationship, let's begin. It's a journey you won't regret.

PART I

The Enneagram

Calling the crowd to join his disciples, he said,
"Anyone who intends to come with me has to let
me lead. You're not in the driver's seat; *I* am . . .
Self-help is no help at all. Self-sacrifice is the
way, my way, to saving yourself, your true self.
What good would it do to get everything you
want and lose you, the real you?"

—*Mark 8:34–36, MSG*

History of the Enneagram

Although the origins of the Enneagram are not exactly clear, scholars have traced the ideas from which it is drawn back thousands of years, through various cultures across the globe and into many of the world's major religions. Some have proposed that a version of the Enneagram diagram may have been used by the ancient mathematician Pythagoras as he considered matters of philosophy and geometry; others hold that early Christian monks' explorations of what inhibits our connection with God informed the system's identification of each type's "core weakness." Ideas similar to the Enneagram's have also been found in Islam and Judaism, which speaks to its resonance with spiritual seekers.

In the West, the use of the Enneagram is relatively new, dating back only 50 years or so. Since then, countless spiritual teachers and human behavior experts have adapted its use, resulting in the version of the Enneagram we use today: an ever-evolving tool that has helped so many deepen their understanding of themselves, others, and God.

THE ENNEAGRAM AND YOUR FAITH

The Enneagram's use in many different faith traditions suggests the universal value of this tool, offering those who are willing to take an honest look into their own souls the ability to truly transform with God's help. As is critical for any kind of spiritual growth, the Enneagram invites us to "examine and probe our ways" so we might "return to the Lord" (Lamentations 3:10) and to God's deeper purposes for our lives. It also invites us to recognize the ways in which we have let a "false self" (or persona, which means "mask" in Greek) lead us instead of partnering with God to be who we truly are. In this book, we will accept the invitation to let God lead us into considering how the Enneagram intersects with and supports the teaching of Jesus's greatest commandment: to love one another as we love ourselves.

I'm assuming you can think of your own examples of how different perspectives on something have gotten you crossways with someone you were in a relationship with, but it reminds me of a story about me, my husband and the kids, and our giant whale of a conversion van in a rainstorm.

It was about an hour into the trip when it began to rain heavily, and because my husband is no stranger to driving in all kinds of weather, I didn't think much of it. Soon, though, I could see that Shane seemed twitchy and irritable. I had seen him navigate storms that were much worse before, so I was a little annoyed when I less-than-lovingly inquired, "What's your problem?"

"I can't see *anything*!" he replied, exasperated.

"What do you mean?" I asked and looked through my own side of the windshield, where the view was clear and the rain was being wiped perfectly from the glass every few seconds. "It's not even raining that hard!"

Even though my response wasn't overtly offensive, albeit in hindsight a little less sensitive than I would like, a tiny smidge of annoyance may have leaked out into what I actually said.

"My wiper sucks!" he shouted, and only then did I make the long lean over to his side of the windshield, where I saw what he meant. He literally could hardly see out of the window at all because his wiper was doing such a terrible job.

I instantly felt terrible about having diminished the struggle he was having. He had been keeping us all safe and on the road in a rainstorm while unable to see clearly. My view was the only perspective I had given any attention to. It seemed fine to me, so I thought it should be fine for him, too.

The gift of the Enneagram for relationships is that it offers us insight into the perspectives of others. It shows us what streaks up their windshields, so to speak, and how that differs from what streaks up our own, and *why*. Knowing that we have a personal way of seeing and that we see everything in our life through that streaky windshield is a game-changer, but understanding the same about those we have relationships with can hand us the keys to understanding and loving one another with infinitely more grace and effectiveness.

How to Use This Book

This book's next two sections will help you familiarize yourself with the Enneagram's structure and the nine Enneagram types, first from your own perspective and then from the perspective of the person you're in a relationship with. Here are some things to remember:

* There is no best or worst type. We are equally gifted in unique ways, and we all struggle.

* Your core type never changes (though people often mistype themselves).

* No one else gets to decide your type. Only you know your deepest motivations.

* Resist the temptation to try to identify others' types. Letting them read about your type in this book may be all the encouragement they need to discover theirs, too.

* You are not your number. You are so much more! The purpose of discovering our core type is so we can grow.

* By that same token, Enneagram type is not a justification for bad behavior. It's a tool to help you awaken to healthier ways of doing things.

* Don't use the Enneagram to attack others. We are all on a journey.

It's my sincere hope that this book deepens and enriches your relationship with yourself, others, and God and helps you realize that though we may see differently, we all possess beautiful gifts that God intended us to use in showing love to each other and the world. May we use the tool of the Enneagram with grace, compassion, and honesty.

In the first part of the book, we'll cover the basics of the Enneagram. The Enneagram's system of nine personality types provides language for what's going on inside you, helps you discover how you see the world, and makes sense of the motivations behind the things you do. Discovering your type, which we'll cover in the second part of the book, helps highlight your unique strengths and potential weaknesses and then gives you personalized strategies for growth. You will develop more self-awareness as you learn to observe your tendencies with nonjudgmental curiosity and partner with God to allow the mask of your personality type to loosen, revealing the beauty of who you truly are.

Once you know your own type, so much insight can be gained by understanding your partner's way of seeing and being in the world, too. This understanding will help you grow together in love. In the book's third section, you will discover more about their type's communication style and learn how to manage conflict with more skill and compassion. You'll discover the truth about compatibility between your two types and how to affirm your partner in the ways they uniquely need. This section will teach you secrets for building strong relationships and loving one another in the most supportive ways.

Enneagram Basics

The Enneagram is a dynamic system that takes into account the fluid nature of our personalities and the uniqueness of every person God created. If you discover that your type is the same as someone else you know but have trouble seeing your similarities, the following concepts can begin to explain why. Like colors in a kaleidoscope, each of us has their own special hue to offer the world.

YOUR CENTER OF INTELLIGENCE

This aspect of the Enneagram relates to how we take in and process information from the world around us. Knowing this about yourself may help you discover your type. Heart-Centered types (Two, Three, and Four) are people who first experience something through their emotions and tend to be more image-conscious. The Head-Centered types (Five, Six, and Seven) tend to receive information through their mental center and tend to process and plan things before they take action. The Gut- or Body-Centered types (Eight, Nine, and One) tend to process life through their gut instincts and to be more direct and honest.

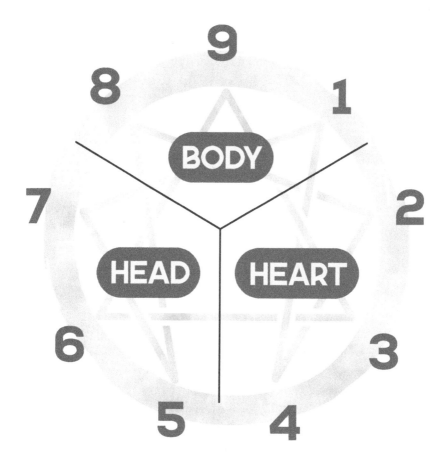

STRESS AND SECURITY NUMBERS

Your stress and security numbers are found by following the lines that radiate outward from your core type on the Enneagram figure. These connection points are important because they explain how your behavior changes in times of stress and when you're feeling secure.

You take on some of the less healthy behaviors of your stress number when you are feeling overwhelmed or under-resourced. For example, a normally relaxed Type Nine may become anxious and reactive when they unconsciously move to their stress number, Type Six. It's helpful to know your "stress move" because those behaviors can alert you (and those who love you) to the fact that you aren't doing well so you can get the extra care and support you need before you break all the way down.

Your security number indicates how you behave when you're growing or feeling secure. For example, a Type Seven who tends to be scattered and unfocused can work to integrate the healthiest behaviors of their connection to their security number, Type Five, for more stability and concentration.

God has created you with these resources already within you. Finding ways to access them will help you live beyond the limiting patterns of your type so you can embody the fullest and freest version of yourself.

INSTINCTS AND SUBTYPES: A DEEPER UNDERSTANDING OF YOUR TYPE

When the core weakness of your Enneagram type combines with your strongest basic instinctual need, a unique focus of attention results. We each have all three of these basic human instincts but tend to give one of them more focus:

- **Self-Preservation Instinct (SP)** relates to matters of personal comfort and security, having enough resources, avoiding danger, and maintaining structure, habits, and well-being for ourselves.

- **Social Instinct (SO)** focuses on belonging to a community or group and the relationships, recognition, and power we gain from membership.

- **Sexual Instinct, also called One-to-One (SX),** focuses intensely on making and keeping connections with specific individuals and bonding with them, sexually and/or through creative energy that projects something of ourselves and our legacy into the future.

Your dominant instinct drives all the behaviors that are associated with your type and results in a more nuanced expression of your Enneagram number. This "subtype" of your Enneagram type is one explanation for why people who share a number on the Enneagram can look and behave so differently, which is especially true of the countertype of each number. Looking at subtypes can also help you get clarity on your type if you're struggling to discover it. A person may talk about their subtype by saying, "I'm a Self-Preservation (type) Two." This is a complex topic explained more thoroughly by expert Beatrice Chestnut in her book *The Complete Enneagram.*

When looking at the Enneagram, wings are the types on either side of your core type. For example, a Type Two's wings are One and Three. Think of wings as handy toolboxes containing strategies and skills for behaving in ways that help you grow beyond your type's stereotypical problems or limitations. Although your motivations and core type never change, the influence of your wings adds flavor and nuance to your unique personality expression. It's an excellent idea to read more about your wings! You may exhibit more behaviors of one wing or the other, depending on the situation and how you are feeling in the moment. By accessing the healthiest aspects of one or both wings, you can break free from the limiting behaviors and pitfalls of your core type and become more integrated.

Self-Assessment for You and Your Partner

Following are groups of 20 questions, each relating to one of the nine Enneagram types. Read each sentence carefully and mark the statements that seem true for you. Don't overthink your answers. They will help you narrow down your type, even if you don't "land" on just one.

When you are finished, tally up how many boxes you checked in each section. Hold your results loosely because assessments are just a starting point for your Enneagram journey. Then read the type basics for the three types you checked the most boxes for (page 18), carefully considering the core motivations for each type to see which sounds more like you. Does one seem to fit more than the others? If so, turn to the chapter for that Enneagram type and see how the information there resonates with you.

If you have lots of check marks, that's okay. The truth is, we have a little of all nine types in us, so keep reading. Discovering your core type may take lots of self-observation, but it's worth the work to begin to truly understand how God made you.

PARTNER 1 PARTNER 2

1. ☑ ☐ I find it hard to relax unless all my work is done.

2. ☑ ☐ I can think much better when my environment is in order.

3. ☑ ☐ I often feel obligated to do the right thing.

4. ☑ ☐ I struggle to resist fixing things that seem wrong to me.

5. ☑ ☐ People have told me they think I'm critical.

6. ☐ ☐ The truth really matters to me.

7. ☑ ☐ Making a mistake is a big fear of mine.

8. ☐ ☐ I have high ideals for myself and others.

9. ☐ ☐ Spontaneity doesn't come naturally for me.

10. ☐ ☐ I tend to think in terms of black and white, right and wrong.

11. ☑ ☐ I rarely feel like I have done enough.

12. ☐ ☐ People don't generally work as hard as I do.

13. ☑ ☐ I have a critical inner voice that's always telling me what I should've done better.

14. ☐ ☐ I am drawn to things that seem perfect.

15. ☑ ☐ People have told me that I'm too hard on myself.

16. ☐ ☐ Matters of injustice really bother me.

17. ☐ ☐ I constantly compare myself to others.

18. ☑ ☐ I am more responsible, dedicated, and detail-oriented than most.

19. ☑ ☐ I feel terrible if I don't do what's expected of me.

20. ☐ ☐ I have a lot of self-control.

11

PARTNER 1
PARTNER 2

1. ☐ ☐ I can often sense what others need before they do.

2. ☐ ☐ I really need to be appreciated.

3. ☐ ☐ Relationships mean everything to me.

4. ☐ ☐ People often tell me how generous I am.

5. ☐ ☐ I have a hard time saying no.

6. ☐ ☐ I can struggle with people-pleasing.

7. ☑ ☐ My own needs often go unmet because I don't know what I want or how to communicate them.

8. ☐ ☐ I'm always afraid I like someone more than they like me.

9. ☐ ☐ I find it easy to give of myself.

10. ☐ ☐ I am warmhearted and genuinely like most people.

11. ☐ ☐ I never want to be seen as needy.

12. ☐ ☐ At the end of the day, I just want to be loved.

13. ☑ ☐ I feel guilty when I'm not able to help someone.

14. ☐ ☐ I have a hard time maintaining my own boundaries.

15. ☑ ☐ I don't like asking for help.

16. ☑ ☐ I really wish I could be everything for everyone.

17. ☐ ☐ I tend to wear my heart on my sleeve.

18. ☐ ☐ Sometimes I use flattery to get what I want.

19. ☐ ☐ My self-worth is very dependent on how I think others see me.

20. ☐ ☐ I long to show love to others and feel loved myself.

4

PARTNER 1 / PARTNER 2

1. ☑ ☐ I love setting and achieving goals.

2. ☐ ☐ I can tend to overwork myself.

3. ☐ ☐ I give a lot of thought to my image and reputation.

4. ☐ ☐ I have a lot of visions for how things could be in the future.

5. ☐ ☐ Being seen as successful is important to me.

6. ☐ ☐ I feel guilty if I'm not being productive.

7. ☑ ☐ I fear failing.

8. ☑ ☐ I have a long list of things I want to do.

9. ☐ ☐ I think feelings get in the way of progress.

10. ☑ ☐ I'm a competitive person.

11. ☐ ☐ It's easy for me to see the potential in others.

12. ☐ ☐ People have told me that I inspire them.

13. ☐ ☐ I always strive to be the best.

14. ☐ ☐ I don't mind cutting corners to get the job done.

15. ☑ ☐ I'm a good team player.

16. ☐ ☐ I secretly long to be loved for who I am, not just what I do.

17. ☐ ☐ I like getting recognized for my accomplishments.

18. ☑ ☐ I am highly competent.

19. ☐ ☐ I often compare myself to others.

20. ☐ ☐ I'm good at hiding my insecurities.

6

PARTNER 1 PARTNER 2

1. ☐ ☐ I often feel misunderstood by others.

2. ☐ ☐ I have a deep appreciation for aesthetics.

3. ☐ ☐ People often think I'm being dramatic.

4. ☐ ☐ I tend to get stuck longing for things to be different.

5. ☐ ☐ I pay a lot of attention to my emotions.

6. ☑ ☐ I tend to want to do things my own way.

7. ☐ ☐ Authenticity is a core value of mine.

8. ☐ ☐ I don't find it uncomfortable to be melancholy, though others seem to want me to snap out of it.

9. ☐ ☐ I tend to push people away to see if they will come back.

10. ☐ ☐ I feel like I'm always searching for my true identity.

11. ☐ ☐ Sometimes I struggle getting over past hurts.

12. ☐ ☐ I spend a lot of time fantasizing about what could be.

13. ☐ ☐ People often admire my creativity.

14. ☐ ☐ I am not like anyone else I know, and I like that about myself.

15. ☑ ☐ I feel like I'm too sensitive.

16. ☐ ☐ I often feel like I'm too much or not enough.

17. ☐ ☐ I feel guilty when I overshare with others.

18. ☐ ☐ My moods are constantly changing throughout every day.

19. ☐ ☐ I'm afraid that I'm ordinary.

20. ☐ ☐ I long to be more balanced, but I don't know how.

2

TYPE FIVE

PARTNER 1   PARTNER 2

1. ☑ ☐ I don't mind being alone—in fact, I like it.

2. ☐ ☐ I often get lost in my thoughts.

3. ☑ ☐ I'm good at holding my own boundaries.

4. ☐ ☐ Often people think I'm aloof or unsociable.

5. ☑ ☐ My independence is very important to me.

6. ☐ ☐ I don't like being intruded upon.

7. ☐ ☐ I tend not to share details about myself.

8. ☐ ☐ I place a high value on privacy.

9. ☑ ☐ I hate being put on the spot and have trouble acting spontaneously.

10. ☐ ☐ I spend lots of time trying to make sense of the world around me.

11. ☐ ☐ I experience guilt when I know I'm being too guarded.

12. ☐ ☐ I feel like I have to carefully manage my time and energy.

13. ☐ ☐ I like to observe life from a distance.

14. ☑ ☐ I fear that I'm not equipped to handle what comes my way.

15. ☐ ☐ I like to collect things that are meaningful to me.

16. ☑ ☐ I'd rather be with a few people than in a large group.

17. ☑ ☐ I need lots of processing time to figure out how I feel about something.

18. ☐ ☐ I feel like I can never know enough.

19. ☐ ☐ I want people to see me as someone who knows what they're talking about.

20. ☐ ☐ It's hard for me to be generous.

7

THE ENNEAGRAM   13

PARTNER 1 / PARTNER 2

1. ☑ ☐ I have a hard time trusting myself to make good decisions.
2. ☑ ☐ I feel good when I'm being productive.
3. ☐ ☐ I don't always trust authority at first.
4. ☑ ☐ I like feeling like I'm part of a group.
5. ☑ ☐ I tend to worry a lot.
6. ☑ ☐ I tend to be very devoted to people or groups that have earned my trust.
7. ☐ ☐ Predictability and consistency make me feel safe.
8. ☐ ☐ People have called me a pessimist, but I think I'm a realist.
9. ☐ ☐ I ask a lot of questions.
10. ☑ ☐ I can't help but think about worst-case scenarios.
11. ☑ ☐ I'm really good at troubleshooting.
12. ☑ ☐ I feel guilty when I change my mind about things.
13. ☐ ☐ I desire to have certainty above all.
14. ☑ ☐ It's hard for me to turn off my brain.
15. ☑ ☐ I really hate getting blamed for things.
16. ☐ ☐ People can count on me for my support.
17. ☑ ☐ I can be overly cautious or take big risks, depending on the day.
18. ☑ ☐ What I really want is to feel safe and secure.
19. ☐ ☐ If I'm feeling anxious, I tend to busy myself with tasks.
20. ☐ ☐ If something is true about me, sometimes the converse is, too.

12

PARTNER 1 / PARTNER 2

1. ☐ ☐ I'm an optimist.

2. ☐ ☐ I love spontaneity and exciting possibilities.

3. ☐ ☐ I hate being bored.

4. ☑ ☐ I feel guilty when I don't have the energy to keep the positivity flowing.

5. ☐ ☐ I think a lot about the future and "what's next."

6. ☑ ☐ I do everything I can to avoid painful situations and feelings.

7. ☑ ☐ I don't like limitations of any kind.

8. ☐ ☐ I have a lot of plans and dreams.

9. ☐ ☐ At the end of the day, I just want to be happy and feel free.

10. ☐ ☐ I can be extremely impulsive.

11. ☑ ☐ I have trouble feeling satisfied and thinking what I have is enough.

12. ☐ ☐ I love new people, experiences, and adventures.

13. ☐ ☐ I tend to be very curious and quick-minded.

14. ☐ ☐ It's hard for me to commit to things because something better might come along.

15. ☐ ☐ I can find a silver lining in any cloud.

16. ☐ ☐ I can tend to fill my plate too full, which makes me seem scattered.

17. ☐ ☐ I have a huge fear of missing out on things.

18. ☐ ☐ I go after what I want, and I usually get it.

19. ☐ ☐ I get distracted rather easily.

20. ☐ ☐ I'm a big-picture thinker, and attending to details is harder for me.

4

PARTNER 1
PARTNER 2

1. ☐ ☐ I like the energy I feel when I challenge people or ideas.

2. ☐ ☐ People have told me I need to "tone it down."

3. ☐ ☐ I get angry easily, but it blows over quickly, too.

4. ☐ ☐ I don't feel guilty about much.

5. ☐ ☐ I am a hard worker, and I think everyone else should be as well.

6. ☐ ☐ I have an iron will.

7. ☐ ☐ I enjoy pushing myself and others to the edge of their capabilities.

8. ☑ ☐ I don't like to seem weak or dependent.

9. ☐ ☐ It really bothers me when people won't stand up for themselves.

10. ☐ ☐ I can offend people with my straightforward, no-BS style.

11. ☐ ☐ I hate being controlled.

12. ☑ ☐ I'm a natural leader, and most others can't lead as well as I can.

13. ☐ ☐ Injustice makes me angry.

14. ☐ ☐ I have big feelings, but aside from anger, I usually keep them hidden.

15. ☐ ☐ I love intensity, but sometimes it's too much for other people.

16. ☐ ☐ I will unapologetically defend the people I love, with force if necessary.

17. ☐ ☐ If I do something, I also have the tendency to *over*do it.

18. ☐ ☐ I have a lot of passion and drive for the things and people I really care about.

19. ☐ ☐ I love to do what others say can't be done.

20. ☑ ☐ I get really angry when I feel disrespected.

3

PARTNER 1
PARTNER 2

1. ☑ ☐ I hate conflict.

2. ☐ ☐ I am an easygoing and basically content person.

3. ☑ ☐ I love to be comfortable.

4. ☑ ☐ I think everyone's point of view deserves to be heard.

5. ☐ ☐ I don't have trouble relaxing.

6. ☐ ☐ It's easy to daydream or let my thoughts wander.

7. ☐ ☐ I don't get too worked up about much.

8. ☐ ☐ I tend to feel guilty if I get my way.

9. ☑ ☐ It's hard for me to say what's on my mind if I think it could cause conflict.

10. ☐ ☐ Sometimes I say yes when I really want to say no.

11. ☐ ☐ Sometimes I feel totally numb.

12. ☐ ☐ I tend to think about the past a lot.

13. ☑ ☐ I can be quietly stubborn.

14. ☑ ☐ I find being in nature very soothing.

15. ☐ ☐ I can fall asleep almost anywhere.

16. ☑ ☐ I'm afraid that who I am and what I think doesn't really matter that much.

17. ☑ ☐ It's difficult for me to make decisions if I think it will make someone else mad.

18. ☐ ☐ People think I am more chill than I really am.

19. ☑ ☐ More than anything else, I long to have peace in my surroundings and inside myself.

20. ☐ ☐ I don't think about myself very much.

9

Core Motivations for Types One to Nine

Now let's check your results. Every assessment test centers on your behaviors, but it's the motivations behind those behaviors that determine your type. For example, two people may describe themselves as "helpful," but one person may be helpful because they believe it's the right thing to do, whereas another may be helpful so they can avoid the conflict they fear will come if they're not. First, some definitions.

* **Core Fear:** what you're most afraid of and want to avoid at all costs

* **Core Desire:** what you believe will solve your problems and make you feel complete

* **Core Weakness:** also called the passion, what keeps you suffering and stuck, inhibiting true connection with God, others, and your true self

* **Healing Message:** the words of truth your heart longs to hear

TYPE ONE: THE PERFECTIONIST

* **Common Traits:** responsible, hardworking, dependable, detail-oriented, ethical, idealistic

* **Core Fear:** being bad, wrong, defective, or corrupt

* **Core Desire:** to be good and pure, have integrity, and do the right thing

* **Core Weakness:** resentment—buried, unacknowledged anger

* **Healing Message:** "You are good."

TYPE TWO: THE HELPER

* **Common Traits:** thoughtful, warm, generous, empathetic, helpful, nurturing, considerate

* **Core Fear:** being unwanted, replaceable, or unloved

- **Core Desire:** to feel loved and appreciated

- **Core Weakness:** pride—believing others need the help only you can provide while denying your own needs

- **Healing Message:** "You are loved for who you are, not for what you do for me."

TYPE THREE: THE ACHIEVER

- **Common Traits:** efficient, successful, productive, driven, image-conscious, motivating

- **Core Fear:** being a failure, being worthless

- **Core Desire:** to be seen as successful, as someone to be admired, as a role model

- **Core Weakness:** deceit—related to your ability to shape-shift and adopt whatever role you need to play

- **Healing Message:** "You are admired for who you truly are, not just for your achievement."

TYPE FOUR: THE INDIVIDUALIST

- **Common Traits:** intuitive, imaginative, inspiring, emotionally sensitive, romantic, intense, attuned to beauty

- **Core Fear:** being defective, insignificant, or mundane

- **Core Desire:** to feel seen, whole, and unique

- **Core Weakness:** envy—a longing for things to be different from what they are

- **Healing Message:** "You are seen and loved as your unique self, and you are whole, lacking nothing."

- **Common Traits:** perceptive, intelligent, innovative, objective, detached, private, self-reliant

- **Core Fear:** being incompetent, incapable, invaded, depleted, or dependent

- **Core Desire:** to be independent, possess knowledge, and have everything figured out

- **Core Weakness:** avarice—striving to retain the resources you possess (time, energy, material things)

- **Healing Message:** "You have abundance and will not be depleted."

KR

————————— TYPE SIX: THE LOYALIST —————————

- **Common Traits:** loyal, dependable, hardworking, faithful, witty, trustworthy, steady, strong

- **Core Fear:** being without guidance or support; fear itself

- **Core Desire:** to feel supported, to have stability and security

- **Core Weakness:** anxiety—a free-floating sense of fears and "what-ifs"

- **Healing Message:** "You are safe and secure."

————————— TYPE SEVEN: THE ENTHUSIAST —————————

- **Common Traits:** spontaneous, excitable, animated, positive, multi-passionate, sociable, curious, engaging

- **Core Fear:** being limited, bored, trapped in pain or sadness

- **Core Desire:** to be satisfied, fulfilled, and content

- **Core Weakness:** gluttony—the pursuit of constant stimulation to overcome or prevent inner emptiness

- **Healing Message:** "You will be taken care of."

TYPE EIGHT: THE PROTECTOR

- **Common Traits:** assertive, honest, direct, self-confident, intense, confrontational, passionate, big-hearted

- **Core Fear:** being controlled, weak, or at the mercy of injustice

- **Core Desire:** to be strong, powerful, and in control in order to protect yourself and those you love

- **Core Weakness:** lust—a desire for intensity, control, and power

- **Healing Message:** "You will not be betrayed."

TYPE NINE: THE PEACEMAKER

- **Common Traits:** thoughtful, accommodating, easygoing, warm, friendly, approachable, understanding, others-focused

- **Core Fear:** conflict; being overlooked, disconnected, dismissed

- **Core Desire:** to experience inner and outer peace and harmony

- **Core Weakness:** sloth—the tendency to be asleep to your own desires and opinions in order to stay comfortable and prevent conflict

- **Healing Message:** "Your presence matters."

> *As each has received a gift, use it to serve one another, as good stewards of God's varied grace.*
>
> **—1 PETER 4:10, ESV**

PART 2

The Enneagram for Understanding Yourself

It is my prayer that your love may abound more
and more, with knowledge and all discernment,
so that you may approve what is excellent,
and so be pure and blameless for the day of
Christ, filled with the fruit of righteousness that
comes through Jesus Christ, to the glory and
praise of God.

—*Philippians 1:9–11, ESV*

THE PERFECTIONIST

How You Interact

As a Type One, you have an incredible vision for how the world could be better, and you work hard to implement your ideas of how everything could improve, feeling your best when you're being productive. You're highly ethical, disciplined, and thorough, and you believe that there is almost always a right way to do everything. Others know they can count on you to do what you say you will do with excellence, so you often find yourself in charge of gatherings or whole organizations. The gifts your personality type offers the world include a strong sense of purpose, an eye for detail, and high ideals.

YOUR COMMUNICATION STYLE

Your communication style reflects a teaching, or even preaching, tone, frequently using words like "should" or "must" to convey your high ideals and opinions to others. Often, your tendency toward black-and-white thinking is evident in your speech, matter-of-factly reflecting what you see as good or bad, correct or incorrect. The people in your life can expect you to be honest and sincere, freely sharing your needs and opinions in a direct manner.

When conflict arises, it's often due to your resentment regarding an unmet (and often unexpressed) expectation you had about how others should have acted. Ones typically have a cruel Inner Critic, who is relentless in telling you all the ways you should have done better, resulting in continual inner conflict. Adhering to the Inner Critic's extremely high standards is what drives your personality, so you tend to feel as though you've never done well enough and never deserve to relax. When you notice your resentment rising, it's usually an indication that you need to rest and to let go of thinking things can only be one way. Take a deep breath and practice giving yourself and the people in your life a lot more grace.

COMMUNICATION TIP

Be aware that others can receive your tone (and even your facial expressions) as critical, even if you feel as though you're just being helpful. Learn to let some things go, and remember, it is not your job to perfect the world.

How You Look in Stress and Security

In stress, you will move toward the unhealthy side of Type Four. You may notice that you begin to embody the behaviors of your less healthy side, becoming more rigid and increasingly resentful of anyone who is having fun while your Inner Critic gets even louder. Everything that needs fixing screams out to be perfected, and you may begin to feel more melancholy and depressed. Overwhelmed by uncharacteristically big emotions, you might begin to lose confidence and to doubt your lovability. When you feel like this, it's a good idea to take a few moments to check in with yourself and compassionately attend to what you need. Being aware of how you react to stress can help you choose how to handle it instead of reacting in ways that could be damaging.

In security, you will embody the healthiest aspects of your type, using your gifts of reform in positive ways, and you will also begin to take on the great qualities that we associate with Type Seven, becoming more spontaneous, more self-accepting, and less critical. You may feel more playful and enthusiastic and be less dualistic in your thinking. In this space, you tend to focus less on what needs fixing and more on what is good and right just the way it is.

Remember that you have access to both the positive and the negative qualities of Types Four and Seven. For example, although Ones tend to access the best parts of Type Seven when they are doing well, it's also possible to take on some of the negative qualities (such as becoming scattered, excessive, or overly playful) with those you're really comfortable with. Those outside your inner circle might never see this side of you, but those closest to you certainly do!

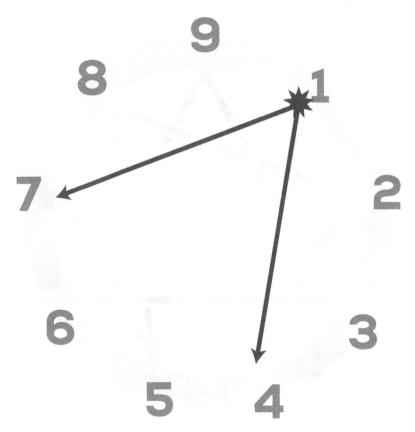

Ones can also take on the wonderful aspects of Type Four, their stress number, when they learn to trust their own intuition, truly experience and even welcome their emotions, and tap into their innate passions and creativity. In this space, you are full of grace for yourself and others, possessing a deep and abiding sense of being loved and acceptable just as you are.

Wings and Subtypes

The way you show up as a Type One can be dramatically impacted by your wings and your subtype, two fluid elements of your personality that may change according to your life circumstances. Using one or both of your wings adds nuance to your type, and the three subtypes represent the various ways your core weakness of anger may be expressed.

WINGS

Ones with a Nine Wing (1w9) are typically more relaxed, cerebral, idealistic, detached, and composed. They have a greater ability to relax and unwind without having to go on vacation.

Ones with a Two Wing (1w2) are typically more helpful, active, empathetic, people-focused, and critical, exuding warmth and gregariousness.

SELF-PRESERVATION (SP)

This type of One feels the most flawed and is the most perfectionistic, expressing anger through working hard to make who they are and what they do more perfect. They worry a lot, look more rigid, have a hard time relaxing, and repress their emotions, judging each one for its appropriateness before allowing it to surface. This One can look a lot like a Type Six because of their tendency to worry and try to anticipate what could go wrong.

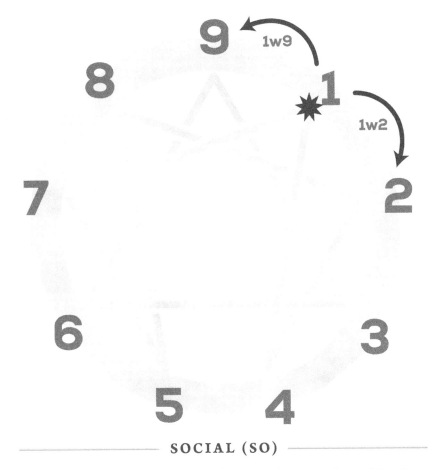

1w9

1w2

9 8 1 7 2 6 3 5 4

SOCIAL (SO)

This One unconsciously sees themselves as perfect, as a role model, and as an example of the "right way" to do and be. They may communicate in an instructive manner and have a "cooler," more intellectual quality about them, like a Type Five. They tend to be controlled and keep their anger half-hidden.

SEXUAL (SX)

Sexual Type Ones are less rigid, can be more impulsive, and focus on perfecting others, feeling entitled to do so because they know better. They don't question themselves as much and use their anger to reform and change what they believe needs to be "righted." This One can look a lot like a Type Eight because they aren't afraid to be angry.

How You Reflect God

You were created with an innate sense of holy perfection, able to see the beautiful potential of everything around you and within you. A strong sense of what is good, right, and pure runs through your veins, which inspires you to reach these heights and achieve these ideals. The most important thing for you to realize, however, is how good and perfect things are already, just as they are. God's grace for the people and things in process on their journey through life is your most important characteristic to cultivate, especially as it relates to you.

YOUR TRUEST YOU

As you begin to accept your own humanness, you will discover that perfection has always been an illusion. No longer will you be limited to a color palette of only black and white, as grace, compassion, and acceptance replace criticism, judgment, and a "one right way" mentality in you. Remember that God created you in love and sees you as being so very good despite any of your shortcomings. Embracing this truth with gentleness and grace will enable you to show up as your authentic self and become a safe person with whom others can be imperfectly themselves as well.

CONNECTING WITH GOD

The ability to be at peace with how things *are*, instead of how they *should* be, is good evidence that you are connected with God and the truest parts of your authentic self. Remember that God sees you as perfect and you are dearly loved, just as you are, despite any flaws you might see. Instead of feeling the need to perfect everything and everyone around you, trust that God is in control and will make divine corrections in the world at just the right time. Be open to the beauty of nuance and the many forms that goodness can take.

God looked over everything He had made; it was
so good, so very good!

—GENESIS 1:31A, MSG

Growing Beyond Your Type

Type Ones are no stranger to self-improvement practices because they often
consider themselves so imperfect. As ironic as it sounds, growth for a One
means you actually need to learn to *not improve*, accepting instead that you
are already good just as you are. Learning to rest more, play more, and let
some things go will help you grow out of your type's patterns and into the
person God made you to be. Being gentle and forgiving with yourself will
enable you to treat others more kindly, too. It's also important that you learn
to recognize the voice of your Inner Critic and notice that it speaks to you
from a place of fear and condemnation. Befriend that part of you and speak
reassurance to it; then turn up the volume on the gentle voice of love, the
still small voice of God. Let it remind you that you are already so good as
you are and worthy of unconditional love, peace, freedom, and rest.

—————————————— BIBLE PASSAGE ——————————————

Come to me. Get away with me and you'll recover
your life. I'll show you how to take a real rest.
Walk with me and work with me—watch how I do
it. Learn the unforced rhythms of grace. I won't
lay anything heavy or ill-fitting on you. Keep
company with me and you'll learn to live freely
and lightly.

—MATTHEW 11:28–30, MSG

2

THE HELPER

How You Interact

Type Twos are uniquely gifted at intuiting what other people need and then giving of themselves to provide help and support. You're warm, affectionate, empathetic, and one of the most people-oriented of all the Enneagram types. You feel your best when your relationships feel solid and when you can help or engage with others in meaningful ways. You get a lot of your identity from how you serve others in order to "earn" their love, and it may feel very uncomfortable for you to acknowledge (or even be aware of) your own needs.

YOUR COMMUNICATION STYLE

As an Enneagram Two, you have a communication style that reflects a sincere desire to connect with others. You're friendly and warm, and you tend to listen with a compassionate ear, asking thoughtful questions and making the people in your life feel heard and valued when they speak. However, your desire to be helpful can make it hard for you not to offer unrequested advice or assistance, thinking you know best what someone else needs. It can be difficult for you to be aware of or communicate your own needs, so it can help for you to check in with yourself periodically to see what you need and whether you can provide it for yourself or ensure the need is met.

<hr/>

COMMON CONFLICTS

Conflicts for Twos can have a lot to do with a lack of boundaries. Because you are kindhearted, you honestly don't mind helping others a lot, until you get tired and begin to feel as if you've been taken for granted. Often, you may tend to "overdo" for others and then feel resentful that the same degree of love and care is not returned to you. Setting limits on how often you say yes is essential, as is accepting that every need you see isn't yours to meet. Having healthy boundaries about how and when you offer help will offer some protection from conflict and the overextension of your love and care.

COMMUNICATION TIP

Most people are not as intuitive as you are when it comes to others, so you'll have to be direct about communicating what you need. Remember, just because someone doesn't know what you need without having to ask doesn't mean they don't love you.

How You Look in Stress and Security

In stress, Twos will begin to take on the less healthy behaviors of Type Eight, becoming increasingly irritable, aggressive, and demanding. In this space, you can tend toward blaming and being controlling or manipulative in an attempt to get what you want. Feeling unappreciated can make an ordinarily selfless-seeming Two power up their anger with surprising force.

In security, Twos take on the great qualities that we associate with Type Four, becoming more nurturing and compassionate toward themselves and more able to accept care and advice from others. In this space, you are more in touch with your own emotions, not just the emotions of others. You're also able to acknowledge the more painful feelings you'd normally try to ignore, such as loneliness, anger, and sadness. This is healthy; attending to your own needs helps you get the support you deserve.

It's important to remember that you have access to both the positive and the negative qualities of Types Four and Eight. For example, although Twos access the best parts of Type Four when they are feeling secure, they can also take on some of the negative qualities (such as becoming too self-indulgent or moody) with people they are really comfortable with.

Similarly, Twos can take on the wonderful aspects of Type Eight, their stress number, when they learn to harness the power and confidence within themselves to bring their gifts of love and care into the world with boundaries and strength.

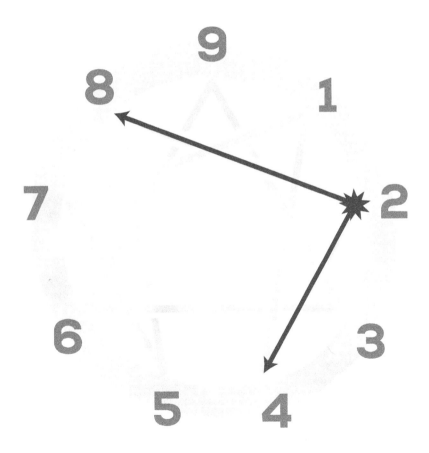

Wings and Subtypes

The expression of your type can be greatly influenced by your wings and your subtype, two elements of your personality that can change according to your environment and what's going on in your life. Your wings can add nuance and flavor to your type, and the three subtypes represent different ways the core weakness of Type Two, pride, can show up.

WINGS

Twos with a One Wing (2w1) are typically more purposeful, judgmental, and concerned with doing things correctly. They have clearer boundaries and are more aware of their own emotional needs. Using your One wing more can help you set healthy boundaries for yourself.

Twos with a Three Wing (2w3) are typically more self-confident, competitive, engaging, and image-conscious. They are almost equally concerned with being successful and being liked. Using more of your Three wing can help you dream and set goals for your own advancement.

SELF-PRESERVATION (SP)

This Two is childlike, youthful-seeming, and unconsciously focused on enticing others to meet their needs without having to ask. Pride is less evident in this version of Two because they are more guarded and need everyone to like them. They are extremely sensitive and more dependent and want to take less responsibility for themselves than other Two subtypes. They can resemble a Type Four because of their emotionality or a Six because of their fearfulness.

SOCIAL (SO)

Social Twos are "adult" in their ambition, their pride being focused on gaining admiration through social connection and having influence on others. They are powerful and responsible leaders who can be quite competitive and strategic, "giving to get" and storing up favors to call in

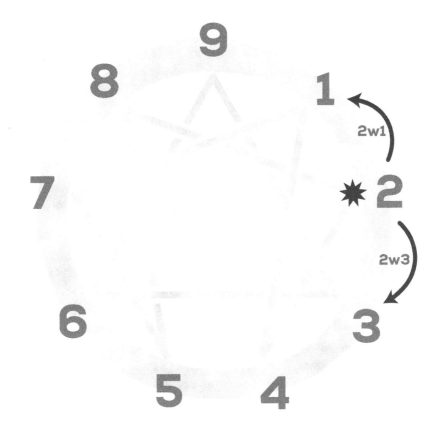

when needed. This Two can resemble Types Three and Eight because of their power and ability to work hard.

SEXUAL (SX)

This Two uses flattery and seduction to win others over and strives to be attractive and appealing to specific others. This fuels their pride and enables them to get their needs met by simply being charming; they also wield a lot of power in relationships. This version of Two inspires the classical archetype of someone who possesses a dangerous beauty, big passions, and emotional intensity.

How You Reflect God

You were created with an innate sense of the love of God and the ability to give compassionately and generously of yourself to care for others. God's love is unconditional and unlimited, and you long for this kind of love to flow freely between all people. Understanding that you are not only a conduit for this love but also deserving of its reception is your biggest lesson to learn. Developing your ability to receive love increases your capacity to give it with wisdom and benevolence.

YOUR TRUEST YOU

When you allow yourself to abide in the love of God, you are connected to the truest parts of who you are. In this space, you will not be ashamed to accept that you were created to receive as well as to give love. You will be attentive to your own needs and even sometimes give them priority over others' needs, knowing that you cannot pour from an empty cup and that you don't have to be "useful" to be worthy. Giving and receiving in equal measure will enable you to experience relationships that feel more mutual, and caring better for yourself will underscore the truth that you are completely lovable.

CONNECTING WITH GOD

As you begin to humbly trust and receive God's love and care, you will let go of the prideful need to give love in order to get it. Your connection with God will be strengthened as you learn to see yourself as beloved, a standing that does not depend on anything you do or any way you help. You are cherished and wanted simply because you're you. Embracing this truth will enable you to give love from a purer place with no strings attached. This is authentic love that flows from the Source of love through you into a world that desperately needs it.

Be completely humble and gentle; be patient, bearing with one another in love.

—EPHESIANS 4:2, NIV

Growing Beyond Your Type

As is true with all of our types, our biggest gifts can become our biggest weaknesses. Learning to use our gifts with discernment is what turns those gifts into the superpowers they were meant to be. This is especially true of your gifts of love. Growth for you will mean that you begin to consider yourself to be worthy of all the love you give others, asking for and accepting help when you need it and caring for yourself instead of waiting for others to notice your needs. You will begin to replace the narrative of needing to be needed with the truth that you can give from a pure place, knowing at the deepest levels of yourself that you are loved and wanted for who you are.

A good practice when you feel compelled to help is to pause and ask yourself if this need is yours to meet or if your meeting it might cost someone else the opportunity to give something. Remember that you weren't meant to carry every burden for those who are hurting. Trust in God's ability to care for all the needs and to give you discernment for where you are truly needed, and you will be the benevolent source of kindness and love you were created to be.

BIBLE PASSAGE

So we have come to know and believe the love that God has for us. God is love, and whoever abides in love abides in God, and God abides in them.

—1 JOHN 4:16, ESV

3
THE ACHIEVER

How You Interact

As a Type Three, you're someone who likes being the best and loves to inspire others to be all they can be, too. You believe that accomplishments are what give you your value, and you feel your best when you're being productive. People know they can count on you to work hard with confidence and competence, smashing goals and crushing to-do lists with ease. Your charm and ambition often gain you admiration, status, and success, which increases the temptation to always present a pleasing image for others. The gifts your personality type offers the world include optimism and the ability to cast a hopeful vision for the future.

YOUR COMMUNICATION STYLE

Your communication style tends to be direct, efficient, and charming, placing a great deal of emphasis on how well you are performing and the image you are crafting. Your superpower is being able to "read" a room and then shape-shift into whatever persona the crowd requires. Sometimes, your goal-oriented focus can make you seem impatient and more interested in your own perspective than others', especially if someone else has a slower pace or is bringing a lot of feelings to the conversation. Even so, your communication style is full of energy that effectively inspires and motivates others.

You can become frustrated when people or circumstances get in the way of what you think needs to be done or when you fear you could fail at what you're trying to achieve. When this occurs, you tend to want to resolve things quickly, sticking to facts and avoiding feelings, believing that feelings will only slow the process even more. Remember that moving too fast can be a way you lose connection with the people in your life (including yourself), and work to train yourself to be present with the situation at hand.

COMMUNICATION TIP

Be aware that your fast pace can sometimes leave others feeling unheard and like you've left them in the dust. For communication success, slow down and check in with the other person, giving them space to process and respond without rushing.

How You Look in Stress and Security

In stress, Type Threes begin to take on the less healthy qualities of Type Nines. In this space, you can become increasingly disengaged, retreating to comfort activities and "numbing out." You may feel very unmotivated to keep up appearances, sometimes even neglecting to take care of yourself. You may feel as though you've lost your confidence and optimism, and you might doubt yourself and your abilities.

In security, Type Threes take on the great qualities of Type Six, becoming more thoughtful and analytical, which enables you to slow your roll a bit. Your cooperative skills bloom in this space, making you wonderfully collaborative within groups. Your cool-seeming exterior warms up a bit as you grow, allowing you to get more in touch with your feelings and who you are under the surface.

Remember that you have access to both the positive and the negative qualities of Types Nine and Six. For example, although Threes access the best parts of Type Six when they are growing, they can also take on some of the negative qualities (such as becoming more anxious, frustrated, and suspicious) with those they are really comfortable with. In the same way, Threes can take on the wonderful aspects of Type Nine, their stress number, by learning to just "be" and incorporating time for healthy rest and relaxation instead of constantly doing, achieving, and performing.

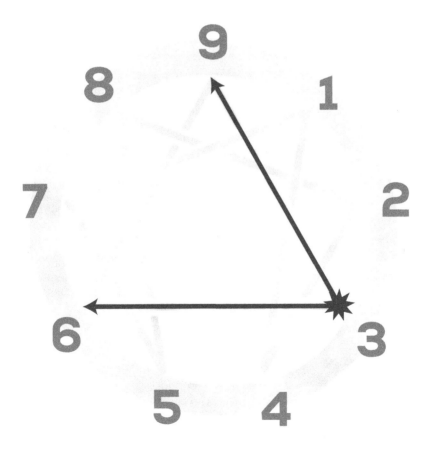

Wings and Subtypes

Your Type Three behaviors can be profoundly influenced by your wings and your subtype, two elements of your personality that can change according to what's happening in your life. Using one or both of your wings adds nuance and flavor to your core type, and the three subtypes represent different ways your core weakness of vanity may show up.

WINGS

Threes with a Two wing (3w2) tend to be charming and entertaining lovers of people with star power. They yearn for appreciation and recognition and can tend toward insecurity. Using more of your Two wing can help you tune in to the feelings of others.

Threes with a Four wing (3w4) are typically more private and emotionally sensitive. This version of Three develops a rich inner life, still focused on achieving success but with more attention to authenticity. Using more of your Four wing can help you get in touch with your feelings and your authentic self.

SELF-PRESERVATION (SP)

This subtype of Three seeks to *be* the ideal model of how a person should be, not just look like it. They don't need to be the center of attention as other Threes do, and they don't feel comfortable openly seeking the admiration of others (though they still want it). Their vanity is about not being vain. They work hard because being productive makes them feel worthy and therefore secure, making them resemble Types One and Six.

SOCIAL (SO)

This subtype is the classic Type Three who wants to get noticed and have influence. They are concerned with competition and winning, climbing the ladder of success, achievement, power, and prestige. Their vanity is channeled into looking good and selling themselves.

SEXUAL (SX)

Sexual Threes are sweeter and less extroverted than the other subtypes of Three. They project an image of desirability and people-please to get what they want, using their charisma and physical attractiveness to gain love. These Threes have difficulty being, feeling, and expressing themselves authentically because they are disconnected from their emotions and their real selves, making them look Two-ish or Seven-ish.

How You Reflect God

You were created with an innate sense of holy hope, able to envision the beautiful potential of everything around you and within you. You have a gift for leading and inspiring others toward a more radiant future and a deep desire to discover what you can offer the world as well. In this way you reflect God's loving plan for everything in creation. Remember that you are valuable and worthy of God's love and affection simply because you're you, apart from anything you can do. No additional achievement can make God love you any more.

YOUR TRUEST YOU

Threes are a part of the heart center, but ironically, they do not access their hearts very easily because they fear attending to their emotions will take too much time. Taking time to get in touch with your feelings is critical, however, to unlocking the most authentic parts of yourself. As you begin to accept that your value lies in who you are, not in what you have achieved, you will rediscover an identity and a self-worth that are based on the image of God in you—your being and not your doing.

CONNECTING WITH GOD

Taking breaks from work to rest, relax, and attend to your feelings will allow you the energy and space needed for real connection with God. This is best done in solitude so you can connect with the truths in your heart without the distractions of needing to be "on" in any way, alone instead with God's love and approval of who you are as God's child. Although spending time alone may be difficult or uncomfortable at first, it's an important practice for you to cultivate so you can replace the lie of "I am what others think of me" with the truth of how innately worthy you are in God's eyes.

You are my beloved; with you I am well pleased.

—MARK 1:11, ESV

Growing Beyond Your Type

It may be surprising to learn that to grow, Type Threes will need to do less and rest more. Often people with your type overwork themselves to the point of exhaustion (even hospitalization) before they will recognize their need to slow down. This is because your identity is so tied to what you do that you may feel as though you're not valuable unless you are accomplishing things. Growth for you will mean learning to trust that you're worthy even when you're not being productive. Remember that your true value comes from being your true self and that living too much as created personas will ultimately leave you feeling empty and disconnected from both yourself and others. Set practical goals for daily rest and you will begin to see the benefits in every area of your life, especially in your relationships. Other evidence of your growth is your ability to be present in the moment, to let go of how others are perceiving you, and to let your emotions come to the surface.

BIBLE PASSAGE

The Lord is my shepherd, I lack nothing. He makes me lie down in green pastures, He leads me beside quiet waters.

—PSALM 23:1–2, NIV

4

THE INDIVIDUALIST

How You Interact

Enneagram Type Fours are deep, creative, and emotional lovers of beauty who tend to experience the full range of feelings every day. People tend to perceive you as intense, sensitive, and genuine, and they know they can count on you to be a great listener when they need one. What you really want is to live with authenticity and to be able to bring your whole self to the world, but you can struggle with sadness around the idea that you're lacking something crucial in yourself that everyone else seems to have. You need help remembering that you're unique, special, and whole, just as you are.

YOUR COMMUNICATION STYLE

Your communication style tends to be expressive and have a lot of intensity. You're an empathetic listener, so people usually find you to be a good conversation partner who is gifted with the ability to hear their struggles without needing to fix them. You tend to talk about yourself and your perspectives freely, but if you are feeling misunderstood, you may become moody, and your communication style may shift so that you seem more withdrawn. Small talk is not your favorite, since you desire to connect at a deep level with people.

--------------------- COMMON CONFLICTS ---------------------

Fours strongly identify with their feelings, and some report feeling as though they don't just have emotions, they *are* their emotions. With your emotional landscape always shifting, it's no wonder that your sense of self can feel unstable to you as well, leaving you feeling as though you're simultaneously too much *and* not enough. This internal struggle may result in external conflict when you feel unseen, misunderstood, or accused by the people in your life, as your narrative about being flawed takes the mental stage. When conflict arises, be aware that your emotional volatility will make it hard for others to reconnect with you, so make efforts to rebalance and ground yourself in what's true, using direct communication to make yourself understood.

================= COMMUNICATION TIP =================

Not everyone can go as deep with you as you would like, but it doesn't mean they don't like you. Be patient and experiment with chatting about the mundane.

How You Look in Stress and Security

In stress, Fours begin to take on the unhealthy qualities of Type Twos, becoming clingy and manipulative and repressing their own needs in order to "earn" love by meeting the needs of others. You may notice that you become increasingly jealous and need lots more affirmation and reassurance from the important people in your life.

When feeling secure, Fours take on the great qualities that we associate with Type One, including becoming more focused. This move enables you to have more discipline in service of your creative pursuits, helping them come alive. Your emotional state becomes calmer and more balanced, allowing for more connection and success in your relationships.

Don't forget, you have access to both the positive and the negative qualities of Types One and Two. For example, although Fours access the best parts of Type One when they are feeling secure, they can also take on some of the negative qualities (such as being judgmental, critical, and stuck in dualistic thinking) with those they are really comfortable with.

In the same way, Fours can take on the wonderful aspects of Type Two, their stress number, when they learn to shift their focus from themselves and their own experiences to seeing, appreciating, and caring for others.

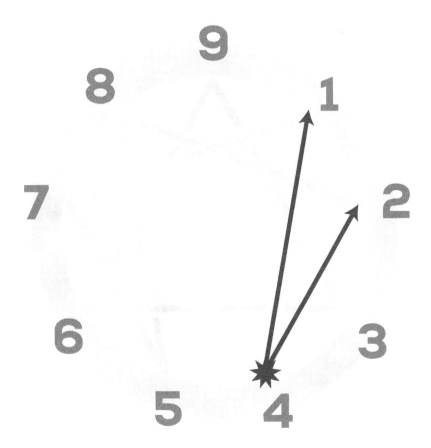

Wings and Subtypes

Your Type Four personality patterns can be directly influenced by your wings and your subtype, two elements of your personality that can change according to your environment and life circumstances. Using your wings can add nuance to your type, and the three subtypes represent the various ways your core weakness of envy can appear.

WINGS

Fours with a Three wing (4w3) are energetic, upbeat, and social. They experience lots of emotional fluctuations, and they care more about what others think of them. Despite this, they are action-oriented and don't mind having more public visibility. Using your Three wing can help you move out of your feelings and get more done.

Fours with a Five Wing (4w5) tend to be more logic-focused, introverted, and analytical. This version of Four is less emotionally reactive, tends to be more intellectual and restrained, and cares much less about what others think of them. Using more of your Five wing can enable you to better discern facts from feelings.

SELF-PRESERVATION (SP)

These Fours want to earn love through their ability to be strong and tenacious. They feel envy toward what they believe they lack (and they think others have) and work hard to get these things for themselves in long-suffering silence. They are more autonomous than other Fours, and their passion for effort bears resemblance to Type Ones and Type Threes.

SOCIAL (SO)

This Four loves social engagement but often feels isolated or marginalized in the midst of it, which confirms their fears that they don't belong. The most sensitive of the Fours, they become very attached to their suffering, feeling as though it's what gives them meaning and uniqueness. This

Four's envy makes them overly focused on what they see as their deep inferiority. They experience guilt and shame over any needs they have and feel as though they are misfits in the world.

SEXUAL (SX)

The Sexual Four's envy is expressed through competitiveness in an effort to get important people to think they're the best. This Four tends to be intense, demanding, and aggressive when they express their needs, and when those needs go unmet, their anger can ignite with a fury. Experts consider this to be the angriest of all the Enneagram types, which is why this subtype can be confused with a type Eight.

How You Reflect God

Type Fours help the rest of us see all the creative beauty of God. Reflecting this beauty, some may offer their special creativity to the world through art, music, story, or simply the way they dress or carry themselves. Fours remind us that God has placed deep meaning into every sacred and ordinary moment and every single one of us, too. Healthy Fours realize that they are wonderfully crafted by God, in beauty and in wholeness, not missing a thing.

YOUR TRUEST YOU

As a Four, you have a deep desire to find your identity and for it to be distinct from anyone else's, often changing aspects of yourself in order to arrive at an idealized version of you but still often feeling as though it's just out of your reach. But have you considered that you are enough just as you are? Understanding that you already belong on days that are ordinary and mundane will indicate that you're in touch with your truest self and the unique essence of who you are. Your truest version of yourself is just waiting to be welcomed by you, and you don't have to do anything besides embrace that belonging to make it true.

CONNECTING WITH GOD

You will find more connection with God as you begin to accept how lovingly and uniquely you've been created. Embracing this knowledge will enable you to return to the deep parts of yourself that understand how much beauty is contained in ordinary moments and people. You'll experience balance and rest as you recognize that there is nothing to prove here; God sees you, understands you, and loves you as you are. A practice of solitude can help you awaken to the nearness and authenticity of divine love and help you learn to rest in your status as a beloved, unique child of God.

You are precious in my eyes, and honored, and I love you.

—ISAIAH 43:4–28, ESV

Growing Beyond Your Type

As you begin to grow beyond your Four-ness, you will be more able to allow feelings to flow in and out without needing to identify with each one of them. This equanimity will enable you to be emotionally honest and balanced, feeling deeply but not getting overwhelmed by your emotions. Instead of needing external validation of your specialness, you will find contentment with who you are as you connect with your heart and with God's view of you as "wonderfully made." Letting go of your tendency to long for more, learning to see what is instead of what's missing, and giving yourself permission to be who you are without comparison to others will be other markers of growth you might notice as you become more self-aware and less limited by the shortcomings of your type. Your relationships with others will benefit greatly from this stability, and you'll be more able to own the truth that you're a unique and whole person who doesn't have to strive to be extraordinary.

BIBLE PASSAGE

I will give thanks to You, because I am awesomely and wonderfully made; Wonderful are Your works, and my soul knows it very well.

—PSALM 139:14, NASB

5

THE OBSERVER

How You Interact

As a Type Five, you're knowledgeable, capable, and inventive. You're a curious learner who craves knowledge and understanding in order to feel secure and competent in the world, but it can sometimes feel as though you'll never know enough. Others see you as intelligent and a source of wisdom, and in fact, many Fives in history have been teachers or visionary pioneers in various fields. Your privacy is important to you, as is always having enough information, energy, and personal space, so you tend to be independent and prefer it when other people are, too.

YOUR COMMUNICATION STYLE

Your communication style could be described as articulate and rational but also one of respectful distance, as you prefer a role of investigator or observer and may tend to take a detached or withdrawn stance. This distance serves you by helping you conserve energy and by allowing you space to run mental analytics, but it can make you seem preoccupied and uninterested, even when you're not. Remember that good communication involves the exchange of words and feelings, so challenge yourself to tune in, engage a little more with others, and share some of yourself, too.

Inner conflict may arise for you when it feels as though people are asking too much or demanding things too quickly from you. This is related to your perception that you must carefully manage your energy stores or else risk being completely drained. Your guardedness may make people in your life feel shut out and cost you the resources others have to offer you if you let them in a bit. Next time conflict arises, see if you can resist the need to withdraw and, instead, feel and share your feelings as they come up. Remember that although time by yourself is important, so is time with others you can trust.

═══ COMMUNICATION TIP ═══

When you need a break from social interaction, be sure to communicate this to your partner; then come back when you've recharged.

How You Look in Stress and Security

In stress, Type Fives take on the less-healthy qualities of Type Seven, becoming scattered, impulsive, and increasingly self-focused. You may have a tendency to come off as rude or condescending, and you begin to cling even more tightly to resources, hoarding them in fear of their depletion in hopes of creating a feeling of security and independence.

In security, Type Fives take on the great qualities that we associate with Type Eight, becoming more decisive, spontaneous, outspoken, and physically present and connecting with their bodies and trusting their instincts. This change in manner is very striking, and it will often surprise people to see Fives showing up with such power and confidence.

Remember that you have access to both the positive and the negative qualities of Types Seven and Eight. For example, although Fives access the best parts of Type Eight when they are growing, they can also take on

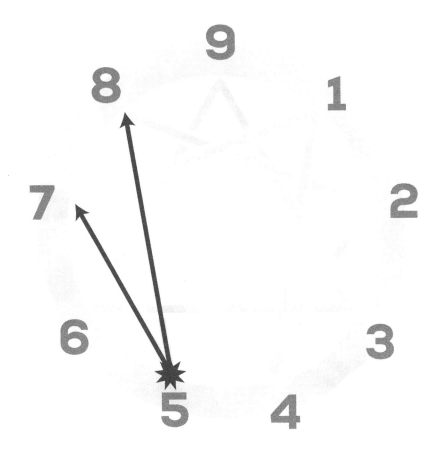

some of the negative qualities (such as becoming very confrontational and argumentative) with those they are really comfortable with. In the same way, Fives can take on the wonderful aspects of Type Seven, their stress number, when they learn to see life as abundant and full of joy with plenty of energy and resources to go around.

Wings and Subtypes

The way you show up as a Type Five can be markedly impacted by your wings and your subtype, two fluid elements of your personality that may change according to your life circumstances. Using one or both of your wings can add nuance to your type, and the three subtypes represent the various ways your core weakness of avarice can appear.

<hr>

WINGS

Fives with a Four wing (5w4) tend to be eccentric, creative, sensitive, emotional, and withdrawn. They may tend to isolate themselves for deep processing of thoughts and emotions. Using more of your Four wing can help you with emotional awareness and expression.

Fives with a Six wing (5w6) typically feel a tension between being collaborative and relational or remaining detached from others. They can tend toward anxiety and skepticism and have great analytical minds, dissecting and solving problems for the common good. Using more of your Six wing can expand your vision to include more perspectives.

SELF-PRESERVATION (SP)

This Five is independent, private, and generally very introverted. They desire to hide in a metaphorical castle and carefully limit their needs and wants in hopes of avoiding being dependent upon anyone else. They have trouble asking for what they want and taking what they need. These Fives demonstrate avarice by creating strong boundaries in order to preserve their resources, protect themselves from the intrusions of others, and remain detached from others.

SOCIAL (SO)

The Social Five is searching for life's ultimate meaning and is avaricious regarding knowledge. They tend to align themselves with people who are extraordinarily knowledgeable experts in their fields, and they are typically more sociable than other Fives, which causes them to bear a bit of resemblance to a Type Seven. According to Enneagram master Claudio Naranjo, these Fives "look toward the stars and care little for life down on earth," preferring the ideal over the ordinary.

SEXUAL (SX)

Sexual Fives are more in touch with their emotions, are highly romantic, and seek to find the ultimate love. It's for this reason that this subtype of Five can be confused with a Type Four. These Fives show less of the core weakness of avarice by softening their boundaries to allow for connection with a partner whom they idealize. Trust is critical in this relationship, and they may experience lots of disappointment as their partner struggles to live up to their expectations.

How You Reflect God

Created with an insatiable thirst for knowledge, Type Fives are a reflection of the depth and truth of God's wisdom. Fives are uniquely wired for curiosity, observation, and investigation, gifts that aid them in their quest to discover answers to the mysteries of the world. Even more remarkable, perhaps, is their ability to absorb and then simplify this knowledge in order to communicate their findings to others, bringing deep knowledge to the surface for us all.

YOUR TRUEST YOU

The essence of who you really are can be found at the intersection of mystery and generosity. Though you possess the ability to search for wisdom like the hidden treasure that it is, growth for Type Fives will look like resting in the knowledge you already have and acting upon that knowledge, even if you don't feel as though you know enough to do so. You will begin to trust others with more of yourself, sharing your knowledge and feelings and letting your mindset of scarcity open up to the abundance of all you are and all that God and His people have to offer, too. You will begin to trust that mystery and generosity lead to more abundance than certainty could ever offer.

CONNECTING WITH GOD

When you are connected with God, you may also notice that you're more connected with your heart space, engaging your emotions as they happen and letting go of your need to be self-sufficient all the time. Learn to turn down your inner noise and become silent and you will find you can trust God's voice of wisdom and care. This will also help you lean in to the mysteries of life without needing to understand them all. Opening your mind and also your heart to give and receive will enable you to experience and embody the generosity of God.

I pray for you constantly, asking God, the glorious Father of our Lord Jesus Christ, to give you spiritual wisdom and insight so that you might grow in your knowledge of God.

—EPHESIANS 1:17, NLT

Growing Beyond Your Type

As inquisitive as Fives can be in discovering things about the outside world, sometimes they can forget to explore the depths of all that they are inside as well. Learning that you are better resourced personally than you realize and embracing the support and connection that's possible when you seek community will show that you are on the path to becoming more of who you truly are. You will begin to trust that you have what it takes to act on all the wisdom you possess, and you will generously share that with others without fear that people will require more of you than you have to give. Your healthy boundaries will enable you to set limits but not be so rigid that you isolate yourself; you'll remember that it's okay to need time for yourself *and* that you need people. Even as you grow in your generosity, you'll find that you'll always be provided with what you need to be secure as well.

BIBLE PASSAGE

God will generously provide all you need. Then you will always have everything you need and plenty left over to share with others.

—2 CORINTHIANS 9:8, NLT

6

THE LOYALIST

How You Interact

As a Type Six, you can tend to be a collection of opposing qualities, meaning that if something is true of a Six, the opposite can also be true. For example, you can be fearful but also courageous, trusting yet distrustful, a person of action who sometimes freezes. You see yourself as a realist, and you are thoughtful, sincere, and witty. You're loyal to trusted people and belief systems, and you generally do what serves the common good. The gifts your type brings to the world include remarkable courage and the ability to troubleshoot and plan for potential issues that could arise in any situation.

YOUR COMMUNICATION STYLE

Your communication style can fluctuate between being hesitant and shy or bold and assured. You tend to ask a lot of questions, and sometimes your communication may have an edge that others perceive as pessimistic or suspicious, but you simply desire to get the full story so you can be prepared to do what you need to do. You tend to be warm and a good listener, but you also need time and space to process your own thoughts. Often the perfect thing to say comes to you after the conversation is over.

People know to listen when you speak because you always have thoughtful perspectives to share.

───────── **COMMON CONFLICTS** ─────────

Sixes live with a lot of inner conflict, thanks in part to an internal committee of voices that challenge them with "what-ifs" and keep them hypervigilant, looking for holes in every choice they make. This can keep you feeling suspicious and anxious and looking for a path to certainty and the guidance you crave. Others may pressure Sixes to make quicker choices or blame them for slowing things down, which only serves to increase the likelihood that conflict will arise. When you feel pressure mounting, take a moment to breathe and communicate your need for some more processing time. Check in with what your gut is telling you and learn to trust your instincts and act on that wisdom.

═══════ **COMMUNICATION TIP** ═══════

> Be aware that although your questions may make you feel more secure, they can have the opposite effect on others, giving them the impression that you don't trust what they are saying.

How You Look in Stress and Security

═════

In stress, Type Sixes can take on the less healthy qualities of Type Threes, becoming increasingly competitive and even arrogant in an effort to project an image of competence as a defense against their anxiety. This anxiety fuels a sense that you need to get busy, which can lead to workaholism. When not doing well, you may also notice you're even more security-minded, expecting worst-case scenarios to come true, hoarding your resources, and being less willing to take any risks.

When feeling more secure, Type Sixes take on the great qualities that we associate with Type Nine, becoming more relaxed and even optimistic. You can trust and empathize with others more easily, and you become less anxious and fearful about life in general. You're more lighthearted, you can see things from more than one angle, and you begin to trust and act upon your gut instincts.

Remember that you have access to both the positive and the negative qualities of Types Three and Nine. For example, although Sixes access the best parts of Type Nines when they're growing, you may also take on some of the more negative qualities (such as shutting down when stressed and feeling irritated when bothered by those in the surroundings) with the people you're really comfortable with. In the same way, Sixes can take on the wonderful aspects of Type Three, their stress number, learning to respect and trust themselves, gaining confidence, and becoming more self-directed.

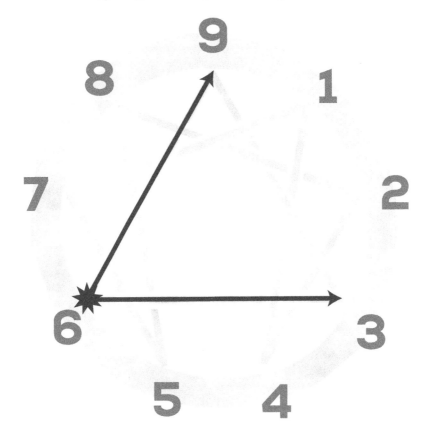

Wings and Subtypes

Your Type Six behaviors can be profoundly influenced by your wings and your subtype, two elements of your personality that can change according to what's happening in your life. Your wing can add a different flavor to your core type, whereas the three subtypes represent the varied ways your core weakness of fear may show up.

WINGS

Sixes with a Five wing (6w5) tend to be knowledgeable, responsible, organized, and serious about what they believe. They can tend toward suspicion but are great advocates for others. Use your Five wing to grow in your self-sufficiency and to help you gain more mental clarity.

Sixes with a Seven wing (6w7) are typically supportive and sociable team players who enjoy having a good time and relish the support of trusted friends. They may be more anxious but also warm and thoughtful. Use your Seven wing to gain a more positive outlook and to have more spontaneous fun.

SELF-PRESERVATION (SP)

The Self-Pres Six is the most phobic Six, whose fear motivates them to create safety by surrounding themselves with friendly relationships. They are warm and friendly but prone to self-doubt, so they lean on others for support and assurance. This can make them resemble Type Twos, but they are more security-focused and less worried about others' approval.

SOCIAL (SO)

This Six acts out their core weakness of fear and creates safety by dutifully adhering to an important group or authority's set of beliefs. They tend to be shy and intelligent, and they love precision, so they can look like a Type One. They may tend toward legalism and dualistic thinking, because certainty makes them feel more secure, and they can also look like a Three because of their love for efficiency.

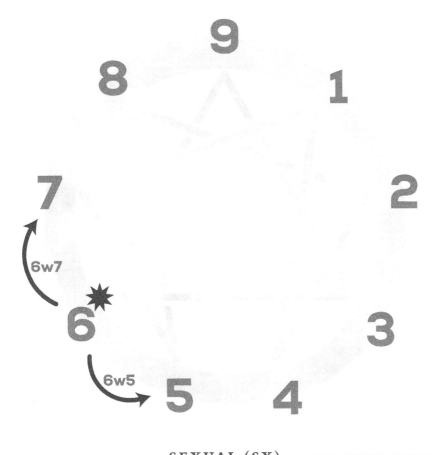

SEXUAL (SX)

The Sexual Six experiences fear and then makes strong moves against it, creating a feeling of safety by confronting dangers head-on. These Sixes can be intimidating, bold, and contrarian, which can make them seem like Type Eights. Their indecision and self-doubt are less obvious in this version of Six because they are action-oriented and move at a fast pace.

How You Reflect God

You reflect the faithfulness of God to the world with a loyal courage that reminds us that we are all thoroughly supported even when things seem uncertain. Your faithfulness is evidenced through your devotion to others and your steady presence. Sixes can struggle to trade their frenzied thoughts for faith-filled trust, but as you do, you inspire others to cultivate trust in God, too. As you walk with courage toward faith in God and let faith in yourself grow, the people in your life will see the beautiful picture of God's fidelity that you present.

YOUR TRUEST YOU

The most authentic version of who you are will emerge as you confront your basic fear of being without guidance and realize that you are fully capable of guiding yourself with the inner wisdom God has placed within you. Practicing silence and working to quiet the internal dialogue of your mind will help you learn to listen and act on what your wise inner voice has to say, thereby gaining self-confidence, becoming more optimistic, and trusting that you can handle anything that comes your way.

CONNECTING WITH GOD

As you loosen your grasp on planning and creating a sense of safety for yourself, you can open more fully to the truth that God will provide what your heart needs most: a deep and abiding presence that will never leave your side. The certainty that you crave can be found in the knowledge that God will guide you in all areas of life. Take time every day to breathe in the truth that God is within you, continually directing your paths and protecting your way. Trusting in that will ignite the courage implanted there by the One whose faithfulness can never fail.

Be strong. Take courage. Don't be intimidated . . . your God is striding ahead of you. He's right there with you. He won't let you down; he won't leave you.

—DEUTERONOMY 31:6, MSG

Growing Beyond Your Type

In order to grow beyond the limiting patterns of your Type Six personality, you will need to realize that safety and certainty are not always in your control. Your ability to plan and prevent problems is a gift, but using this ability more wisely and less reactively will help you experience the peace you really crave. You will learn that you can give yourself a break, instead of thinking you're responsible for everything and doubting that others have done their homework, and trust that everything will turn out okay even if it doesn't all go according to (your) plan.

Trusting yourself and your gut instincts will also be indications that you are growing. You will often find it less necessary to seek counsel outside yourself, leaning instead into your own inner authority and the knowledge of God's faithful provision. Your suspicions and fears of getting blamed for something going wrong will begin to give way to hope and optimism for a future that was meant to be enjoyed.

BIBLE PASSAGE

"For I know the plans I have for you," says the LORD. "They are plans for good and not for disaster, to give you a future and a hope."

—JEREMIAH 29:11, NLT

7

THE ENTHUSIAST

How You Interact

You are a charming and excitable type of person who likes to look on the bright side and is always up for a spontaneous adventure. You love to spend time anticipating new experiences and planning for what's to come, and your future-focused mindset makes you extremely innovative and creative in the employ of your wide range of talents and gifts. You can get into trouble, however, by overbooking your schedule and juggling too much, leaving you feeling scattered. You tend to see life as an endless buffet full of delicious possibilities, and you desire to taste and experience them all.

YOUR COMMUNICATION STYLE

Your communication style brings lots of energy to any conversation. Sevens are animated storytellers who like to jump to the most exciting parts first and keep others' attention with their engaging enthusiasm. Be aware that your excitement can feel intense to other people and that long stories told out of sequence can be hard for others to follow. For better communication, try slowing down and listening more than you talk, asking questions of others, and sharing the most important parts of stories with a bit less detail.

One way conflict may arise for you is when you spread yourself too thin, not wanting to miss out on any opportunities but then being unable to meet all your obligations. This may result in you forgetting details, missing appointments, or being late for events because you've overscheduled yourself. When conflict arises, your ability to stay open to different perspectives will enable you to move through it with understanding and a good attitude. Notice your tendency to make a joke or put a positive spin on things, and make sure you're not doing so in an attempt to shirk responsibility or avoid the discomfort of the situation.

COMMUNICATION TIP

Make sure you're bringing others along as you communicate. A good way to do this is to tune in to the other person by asking them questions.

How You Look in Stress and Security

When feeling stressed or under pressure, Type Sevens take on the less healthy qualities of Type Ones and become increasingly perfectionistic and pessimistic, noticing all that is not good in the world. This leads to judgmental and critical thoughts and speech toward others and yourself, as you become less possibility-minded and more dualistic in your thinking. You may also find yourself getting resentful of others for standing in the way of you having fun.

When doing well and feeling secure, Type Sevens take on the great qualities that we associate with Type Five, becoming more interested in contributing than in consuming. You might find a new ability to tap into your serious side and feel more comfortable with silence and solitude, which allows you to recharge your energy stores. Here, you allow yourself time to think about the meaning and purpose of your life, which can help you find the sense of satisfaction you long for.

Remember that you have access to both the positive and the negative qualities of Types One and Five. For example, although Sevens can access the best parts of Type Five when they are growing, they can also take on some of the negative qualities (such as becoming withdrawn and stingy with their energy) with those they are really comfortable with. In the same way, Sevens can take on the wonderful aspects of Type One, their stress number, becoming more focused, grounded, principled, and able to imagine the highest of purposes for their lives and gaining the discipline to make their big ideas come to fruition.

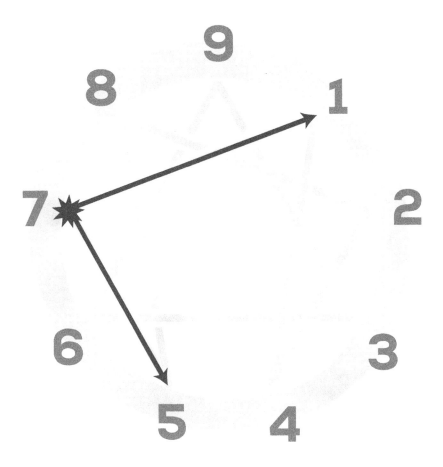

Wings and Subtypes

The way you show up as a Seven can be incredibly impacted by your wings and your subtype, two fluid elements of your personality that may change according to what's going on in your life. Your wings can add a nuance to your type, and the three subtypes represent different ways a Seven's core weakness, gluttony, may be expressed.

WINGS

Sevens with a Six wing (7w6) tend to be charming, outgoing, and loyal, bringing more focus and sobriety into relationships and tasks. They experience a bit more anxiety about what others think of them. Use your Six wing to get realistic and make well-thought-out plans.

Sevens with an Eight wing (7w8) are typically bold, ambitious, and less concerned with what others think. They are confident and innovative, intense but playful. Because they bore easily, they may tend to start things they don't finish. Use your Eight wing to help you make decisions and set good boundaries for your yesses.

SELF-PRESERVATION (SP)

This Seven is charming and friendly, even flirtatious. They create a network of alliances that they can strategically use to their advantage, and they always have their senses attuned to gaining opportunity for themselves. Their gluttony is evident in material ways and in their preoccupation with the pursuit of pleasures of all kinds. These things give them a sense of safety and keep their emotions from surfacing.

SOCIAL (SO)

The Social Seven goes against their gluttony by avoiding focus on their own self-interest and instead sacrifices themselves on behalf of the group. This can make them resemble a Type Two. They are idealistic and often engaged in acts of service as a way to prove they are a "good person," which

can make them look like a Type One. Ultimately, this Seven craves the safety they get from working hard and being recognized for it.

SEXUAL (SX)

Sexual Sevens are imaginative, talkative, suggestible people who are gluttons for idealized and ethereal things. As such, they struggle with things that are ordinary or mundane, preferring to fantasize so they can escape what's painful. These Sevens tend to be humorous and keep very busy, wanting to "do it all," and they feel most secure when they are dreaming about exciting possibilities and opportunities.

How You Reflect God

You were created with the joy of God in your heart and the truth of unlimited possibility and potential for a world restored to the Divine. Your curious energy reminds us of all the things there are to appreciate about our beautiful and fascinating world and that we should make time to experience everything we can. With upbeat positivity and a sincere zest for life, Sevens reflect an excellent example of how looking for the good in every situation can train our perspectives toward God's joy in the present moment and in what's yet to come.

YOUR TRUEST YOU

You can know that you are connected to your truest you when you're confident in your own path, welcoming of your deeper emotions, and grounded in the present moment. Although it is true that you were created with the ability to do *so* many things, you have to face the fact that you can't do *every*thing. This can make you feel as if you are missing out, but as you uncover more of your true self and encounter the desires of your own heart, you'll become more able to let go of what's not for you right now. This focus will help you put your energy and attention on the meaningful things that *are* meant for you. In order to do this, you may need to embrace more of the feelings you'd rather avoid and things that are painful or heavy because they probably contain valuable data about how you can have your biggest impact on the world.

CONNECTING WITH GOD

Presence, gratitude, and a slower pace will help you find your connection with God. Here, you can find safety to feel and heal the sadness you're afraid of, allowing for the full expression of your human emotions. This secure connection will help you trust God to bring you the opportunities your heart desires and the discernment to know which ones are meant for you without needing to fill up on a lot of not particularly meaningful experiences. Remember that, one day, all suffering will pass away, and ultimately you will be provided with everything you need to feel the deep satisfaction you long for.

> *For he satisfies the longing soul, and the hungry soul he fills with good things.*
>
> —PSALM 107:9, ESV

Growing Beyond Your Type

When you are doing well and growing, you will remember to stay present and savor the here and now, knowing that maintaining good limits is healthy.

This will help you truly and deeply experience and appreciate all that life has for you as well as reduce conflict with others. The tendency to avoid anything that brings deeper, sadder feelings will be replaced with the truth that real life is made up of good and bad and in-between and that this is a part of the adventure of being human. Though the temptation to get caught up in overplanning will always be with you, continue training yourself to take a pause to practice rest and silence, which will calm your ever-swirling mind and help you realize that all you really need is right here in the present moment. It may be helpful to repeat this mantra to yourself daily: "I will never miss out on anything that was truly meant for me."

BIBLE PASSAGE

> *You make known to me the path of life; in your presence there is fullness of joy; at your right hand are pleasures forevermore.*
>
> —PSALM 16:11, ESV

8

THE PROTECTOR

How You Interact

Type Eights are the most energetic of all the Enneagram types, and because of all this energy and power and your drive to stand firm in what you believe, you also tend to be one of the most misunderstood. Your strength is certainly felt by others when you are standing against them, but it's especially inspiring to see you use your strength of character and huge heart to protect and care for those in need. Your abundance of passion, quick mind, and amazing stamina enable you to overcome most any challenge and make big things happen.

YOUR COMMUNICATION STYLE

Your boldness and confidence make you a natural leader, and when you talk, people listen. You bring a lot of energy and a "tell it like it is" approach to conversations, expressing your opinions freely and honestly and appreciating it when others do, too. Keep in mind that people can experience you as more demanding and forceful than you intend to project, so it will benefit you to develop your listening skills and stay tuned in to how you're being received, making adjustments to your approach when needed.

Most Eights don't fear or avoid conflict, both because you see it as a means of moving forward and because this kind of intensity makes you feel alive. This can have you jumping into conflict or even creating it when you see an injustice you can do something about. Remember that you have easy access to the emotion of anger, which can be a force for good when used with discretion and discernment or have more destructive consequences when it is allowed full rein. Take the time to get curious about what is underneath your anger to see if there is a deeper emotion that needs attention—sadness, for example—and learn to let more things go.

COMMUNICATION TIP

Though you pride yourself on being direct and honest, be aware that you might get further with others if you soften your approach a bit.

How You Look in Stress and Security

In stress, Type Eights tend to take on the less healthy qualities of Type Five, becoming increasingly withdrawn and disconnected from their own emotions and bodies to the point of being neglectful of self-care. Your fear of betrayal may increase, too, as you become hypervigilant about potential attacks and get more uncompromising in your positions.

When feeling secure, Type Eights take on the great qualities that we associate with Type Two, becoming more caring and letting their sweet side show. You not only give care, but in this space you can receive it, too, trusting others more and revealing your own vulnerability. You become more open to others' opinions and realize that it's not all up to you to protect and ensure justice for all.

Remember that you have access to both the positive and the negative qualities of Types Five and Two. For example, although Eights access the best parts of Type Two when they are growing, they can also take on some of the negative qualities (such as needing a lot of reassurance and requiring more appreciation for the things they do) with those they are really comfortable with.

In the same way, Eights can take on the wonderful aspects of Type Five, their stress number, when they become humble enough to admit that they need time and rest to recharge and care for themselves. In this healthy space, Eights can observe life from a less defended position and gain great wisdom.

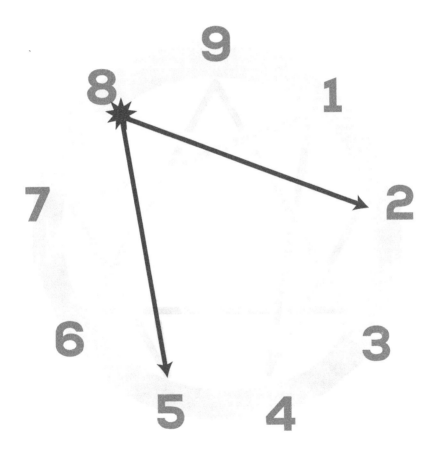

Wings and Subtypes

Your Type Eight behaviors can be greatly influenced by your wings and your subtype, two elements of your personality that can change according to what's happening in your life. Your wings can add a different energy to your type, and the three subtypes represent different ways an Eight's core weakness of lust may show up.

WINGS

Eights with a Seven wing (8w7) tend to be energetic, confident, and aggressive. They are a powerful and driving force intent on making things happen, often in service of others. They may struggle with impatience, impulsivity, or a lack of compassion when not doing well. Use your Seven wing to help you look on the bright side.

Eights with a Nine wing (8w9) tend to be gentle, steady, and strong. Less overtly aggressive, they crave comfort and harmony but will use their assertiveness when needed. These Eights are both softhearted and intimidating, passive and bold. Use your Nine wing to help you choose your battles.

SELF-PRESERVATION (SP)

This Eight pursues what they think they need to survive with power and aggression, if necessary. They are extremely self-reliant survival experts who demonstrate their core weakness of lust by going against rules or people in the way of their satisfaction. The least expressive of the Eights, this type tends to have a quiet strength and might seem cold and distant, looking a bit like a Type Five because of their guardedness.

SOCIAL (SO)

The Social Eight is the Eight that doesn't look like a typical Eight, being more friendly and less overtly rebellious. This Eight uses their lust and aggression in service of other people, but they can have a blind spot related

to their own need for protection and love. For this reason, they can sometimes be confused for Type Two or Type Nine.

SEXUAL (SX)

Sexual Eights are the most emotional of this type and are deeply confident, expressing their core weakness of lust in their passionate, open rebellion against the cultural and societal norms they disagree with. They are often outspoken, magnetic, and attractive, which helps them gain influence over others. This Eight seeks to establish dominance over their environment and can be possessive and impulsive.

How You Reflect God

As a Type Eight, you embody God's power and protection as you champion, defend, and take healing action on behalf of others. Your strength is unmistakable, but your huge, tender heart is the place from which your true power emanates. This, coupled with your love of justice, fuels your passions and makes you a truly inspiring protector of the innocent and the downtrodden.

YOUR TRUEST YOU

The most authentic version of you will shine forth when you let the protection of your personality's traits fall away, trusting others with more of yourself and becoming less wary. This will allow you to become more collaborative with others, allowing you to shoulder less of a burden and giving you the opportunity to listen and learn from others' perspectives without feeling challenged to defend your own stance. The people in your life will respect you even more for your ability to connect with them at a deeper and more generous level.

CONNECTING WITH GOD

In order to connect with God, it is necessary for you to voluntarily lay down your control and all illusions of invincibility and let God be your protector. Resting in divine protection will enable you to access your own innocence and embrace your vulnerability as a created being. Make time to sit in stillness and allow your heart to speak to you, even if that feels weak. It is this "weakness" that is actually your biggest strength and source of power. Remind yourself that you're in God's care, and you don't have to always be the strong one.

> *But [the Lord] said to me, "My grace is sufficient for you, for my power is perfected in weakness." Therefore I will boast all the more gladly in my*

weaknesses, so that the power of Christ may rest on me.

—2 CORINTHIANS 12:9–10, NIV

Growing Beyond Your Type

You will know you are growing beyond your Type Eight tendencies when you can allow your more vulnerable emotions to come to the surface without feeling as though you're being weak and you are able to appreciate your softer side and your humanness. This will come as a result of learning that your true strength resides in your ability to be vulnerable and transparent. Developing more compassion and care for yourself will result in you using more of your strength in service of others with inspiring generosity and kindness.

Other signs of transformation are an enhanced ability to listen and be more patient. You will notice that you can pause before acting on your gut instincts, thinking carefully about the impact of what you might say or do. You'll also be less ashamed of asking for help, trusting others to care for you and even take the lead from time to time. Growing in these ways will provide you with a fuller and more vibrant experience of life and will infuse all your relationships with the honesty and fortitude you truly desire.

———————————— BIBLE PASSAGE ————————————

Those who wish to boast should boast in this alone: that they truly know me and understand that I am the Lord who demonstrates unfailing love and who brings justice and righteousness to the earth, and that I delight in these things.

—JEREMIAH 9:24, NLT

THE PEACEMAKER

How You Interact

Enneagram Type Nines tend to be easygoing, adaptable people who enjoy being comfortable and prefer to avoid conflict. For this reason, you are known as the Peacemaker, constantly trying to maintain a sense of peace in your inner and outer worlds, making sure you calm any waves that come your way, and trying your best not to make any yourself. You tend to be very thoughtful, unselfish, and flexible, and you have a natural ability as a mediator because of your ability to see all sides of things.

YOUR COMMUNICATION STYLE

You are approachable, friendly, collaborative, and invested in promoting connection between people, so you are good at leaving space for others to feel heard. People like to talk to you and see you as a good listener because of this, but at times you can seem as though you're not engaged or paying attention (and sometimes, you really aren't!). Practice speaking up and sharing a bit more in conversations to show yourself and others that you have good insights, too, and to create more of the authentic connection you really desire.

If you're a Nine, chances are you dislike conflict and try to avoid it if at all possible, believing that it could destroy the harmony of your relationships and create the potential for disconnection. Ironically, though, your avoidance of conflict can sometimes be what *causes* conflict, especially as it relates to communicating your own needs and desires. By "going along to get along" instead of voicing your thoughts, you may begin to feel secretly angry about being overlooked by others, even if the reason you weren't considered is because you didn't speak up. Learning to recognize these feelings when they arise, asking yourself what you need, and then communicating these needs can actually help you avoid conflict and connect with the people in your life.

COMMUNICATION TIP

Be careful of what you are agreeing to. Nodding your head in the affirmative may signal to others that you have said yes to something you didn't plan to.

How You Look in Stress and Security

In stress, Type Nines begin to take on the less healthy qualities of Type Six. You may become increasingly anxious and worried, overcommitting yourself and becoming more irritable and emotionally reactive. Self-doubt grows, and you have trouble making decisions due to overwhelming mental stress.

When you are doing well and feeling secure, Nines tend to take on some of the great qualities we associate with Type Three, gaining confidence and assertiveness, taking control of their lives, and living according to an agenda that matters to them. In this space, Nines can experience genuine peace and harmony because they have woken up to the truth that their voice matters.

Remember that you have access to both the positive and the negative qualities of Types Six and Three. For example, although Nines access the best parts of Type Three when they are feeling secure and growing, they can also take on some of the negative qualities (for example, engaging in busywork in order to avoid doing more important things and boasting about their superiority) with those they are really comfortable with.

In the same way, Nines can take on the wonderful aspects of Type Six, their stress number, using their analytical skills more effectively and mobilizing their inner courage to take action on their own behalf.

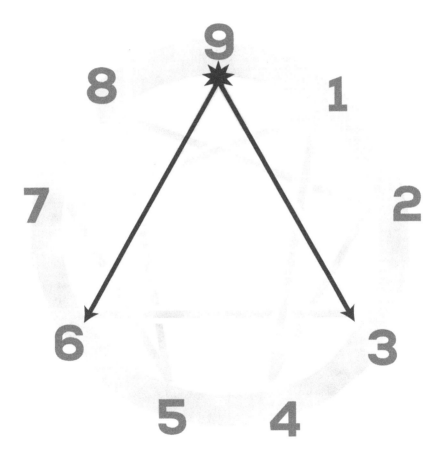

Wings and Subtypes

How you show up as a Type Nine can be greatly influenced by your wings and your subtype, two elements of your personality that can change according to your life's circumstances. Your wing adds flavor and nuance to your type, and the three subtypes of Type Nine represent different ways a Nine's core weakness, sloth, might be exhibited.

WINGS

Nines with an Eight wing (9w8) tend to be expressive, independent, and less laid-back, often having a powerful temper when they are pushed too far or feel overlooked. They are both gentle and powerful. You can use your Eight wing to get into your power and assertiveness.

Nines with a One wing (9w1) are supremely invested in doing what's right for everyone. Justice-oriented and fair-minded, they can be critical and perfectionistic at times. You can use your One wing to access what really matters to you.

SELF-PRESERVATION (SP)

Sloth is expressed through laziness in connecting with themselves and their power, preferring to "lose themselves" by merging with physical comforts and repetitive activities. The Self-Pres Nine is sometimes called the Eight-ish Nine because they are more embodied and have more presence than other versions of Type Nine. They tend to be jolly and loving, though they may not feel loved in return, and they can be quite stubborn and erupt into anger unexpectedly.

SOCIAL (SO)

The Social Nine can be mistaken for a Type Three because they have a lot of energy used in service to the groups they value. They work hard, "fusing" with the desires of this group, often sacrificing generously to earn their place within it and forgetting their own needs and desires along the

way. These Nines are lighthearted, outgoing, and generous, and they make excellent leaders with their unselfish and inclusive approach.

SEXUAL (SX)

This gentle, shy version of Type Nine expresses their sloth by merging with the energy of another person. They are not connected to their own passion for living and find it more comfortable to "be" through another. As a result, they are uncertain about their own identity and find it hard to take action, even if they know what they want. This Nine can look like a Type Two because of their repressed sense of self or a Four due to their tendency toward melancholy.

How You Reflect God

When you are embodying the healthiest aspects of Type Nine, you reflect the peace of God and the holy interconnectedness that makes all things One in Spirit. You remind us that every person has a valuable perspective, and you work to create space for others' voices to be heard. Your calm presence reminds us to rest in the truth that God will ultimately restore all things, bringing the fullness of unity, harmony, and peace to the world.

YOUR TRUEST YOU

As a Nine, you are wired to easily connect and even "merge" with others, but your true self cannot arise until you give yourself some attention, too. Check in daily with yourself to ask what you want and what you don't want; then honor these desires, letting go of the fear that you will be at odds with others if you assert yourself. The people in your life want the real you, so it will actually benefit your relationships if you can awaken to whom God made you to be and then share more of who you are.

CONNECTING WITH GOD

Many Nines find experiencing nature to be a great way to connect with God. Getting outside, going for a walk, and seeing God's beauty on display in creation can connect you with the presence and peace you crave. Think about how everything in nature has its place and its purpose, and then meditate on the truth that you have an equally important place in nature as well. You are God's beloved child, and it brings God glory when you awaken to yourself and bless others with the abilities you have been given.

> *For we are his workmanship, created in Christ Jesus for good works, which God prepared beforehand, that we should walk in them.*
>
> **—EPHESIANS 2:10, ESV**

Growing Beyond Your Type

Type Nines begin to grow when they wake up to their own lives and the unique gifts they were given in order to bring to the world. As you let go of the limitations of your type and claim your true identity, you will begin to see conflict as a necessary part of making things happen and realize that it doesn't have to result in disconnection from others. This new awareness will help you take action to honor your desires and dreams, recognize how much your voice matters, and experience the satisfaction of being engaged in life rather than numb to it.

To show up for your own life, you'll need to assert yourself more and use your abilities to *make* peace, which requires effort, instead of just *keeping* peace. This will require that you acknowledge your feelings of anger and understand that anger can have important, positive effects in the world, such as propelling you to act in service of justice and your passions, which will help you reclaim a healthy sense of self and rediscover your own self-worth.

─────────────── **BIBLE PASSAGE** ───────────────

I am leaving you with a gift—peace of mind and heart. And the peace I give is a gift the world cannot give. So don't be troubled or afraid.

—JOHN 14:27, NLT

PART 3

The Enneagram for Understanding Your Partner

A new command I give you: Love one another. As I have loved you, so you must love one another.

—John 13:34, NIV

THE PERFECTIONIST

Understanding Your
Type One Partner Better

We love Ones because we know we can count on them to be responsible, do what is right, and somehow make everything just a little bit
better—but did you know that they feel as though it's their job to fix
everything that's wrong in the world? Or that they feel that they're never
good enough? Your encouragement and support as their partner can
make a huge difference in helping them realize the innate goodness of
who they are, imperfections and all, which will help them grow beyond
their type's patterns into a more authentic version of themselves.

LIES ONES BELIEVE

Knowing the narratives that your partner believes about themselves
can help you understand and support them. Most of all, it can help
you know what truths to affirm in them so they can grow past their
type's limitations.

LIE #1: **If I'm not perfect, I'm no good at all.**
Ones are both gifted and cursed with being able to see the improvements that could be made, and this makes them especially hard on themselves. Remind them of the truth that they are *good* and that they don't need to be perfect to be loved.

LIE #2: **It's not okay to rest until all the work is done.**
The truth is, there will always be more work to do. Even God rested at the end of a long day of creation. Encourage your One to take breaks for fun and lighten their load by lending your efforts to the jobs that need doing.

Loving Your Partner Well

Your Type One partner may seem as though they can handle anything, but they can really benefit from lots of affirmation from you to offset the negative messages they get from their Inner Critic. Like an unforgiving judge, this voice finds something wrong with most everything your One does and says, and it has so much sway in their thinking that it sometimes may feel that there are three people in your relationship. Your most important job is helping your partner stand up to what the Inner Critic says by pointing out all the ways they are doing well and guiding them to embrace the truth of how much grace God has for them.

COMMUNICATION STYLE

Ones tend to be direct and clear in their communication, and you may notice that they use words such as *should* and *ought to*, evidence of their belief that there is almost always a right way to do something. The dualism of things being right or wrong, good or bad, shows up in their speech, as does a real desire to be appropriate and correct. Sometimes this makes Ones seem rigid, critical, or preaching. Ones can benefit from a partner who helps them see more shades of gray and recognizes their need for support when they get critical or resentful.

Instead of assuming you know how your One is feeling, consider asking them if something is bothering them or if they could use your help. This will help them feel seen and cared about.

NAVIGATING CONFLICT TOGETHER

Because Ones are constantly aware of all the things that need fixing around them, they can sometimes live in a constant state of irritation and anger without realizing it. This can make them outwardly critical and lead to conflict in their relationships when these feelings spill out onto the people in their lives. Being the object of criticism can ignite conflict as well because your One already feels overwhelmed by all the things they feel they must control and is working hard to be above reproach. You can defuse these situations by offering grace and encouragement, lending them help with the work they have to do, and finding ways to break the tension with playfulness.

IT'S NOT PERSONAL

Don't take it personally if a Type One corrects you. Remember that from their perspective they can't help but see what needs improving and telling you how you could be better feels to them as though they are showing you love. See if, instead of reacting to their criticism, you can let them know that you appreciate that they want to help you improve and then gently communicate how their criticism makes you feel. Ones face harsh criticism from their Inner Critic; it may be possible to connect over that feeling.

Practical Tips for Your Type Combination

Although there is no best combination of Enneagram types, using Enneagram wisdom will provide you with a new, shared language for navigating the struggles and triumphs of being together and specific ways to love each other well. Commit to learning about your own type and then use the practice for your type combination to grow together. Remember, your Type One needs you to remind them every day that they are doing better than they think they are and how intrinsically good God made them.

Helpful practices for every type in a relationship with a One:

* *If you're a One:* Take breaks to play together even before the work is done.

* *If you're a Two:* Encourage your One with loving words and accept theirs for you.

* *If you're a Three:* Set goals together for rest and play.

* *If you're a Four:* Encourage your partner to share their true feelings and let them help you balance yours.

* *If you're a Five:* Wonder together about all there is to know and all that isn't simply black or white.

* *If you're a Six:* Find ways to be spontaneous and have fun together.

* *If you're a Seven:* Honor their need to be responsible, and then help them make time to play.

- *If you're an Eight:* Take turns being in charge, laugh together, and work toward common goals.

- *If you're a Nine:* Enjoy nature together, and encourage your One to get the rest they need.

Surely your goodness and love will follow me all the days of my life, and I will dwell in the house of the LORD forever.

—**PSALM 23:6, NIV**

2
THE HELPER

Understanding Your
Type Two Partner Better

To know a Two is to love a Two because they are warm and generous in the ways they give of themselves and love us, but did you know that they often give their love in hopes that they'll receive love from you in turn? Or that, although they are remarkably attuned to what others want and need, they usually need help figuring out what *they* are thinking and feeling? As their partner, you are uniquely positioned to support and encourage them so they can grow beyond their type's pitfalls and into the person God made them to be.

LIES TWOS BELIEVE

When you understand the narratives that your Type Two partner believes about themselves, you can support them in the exact ways they need with truth and grace.

LIE #1: **If I'm not helpful and loving, you won't want me.**
The truth is, we do love the ways Twos care for us, but the more you can reassure them that you love them for who they are rather than what they can do for you, the better. Look for intentional ways to show appreciation for attributes of your Two's character, appearance, or presence in your life.

LIE #2: **If I have too many needs, you'll think I'm too much and abandon me.**
It's a big deal when a Two shares a need they have with you. When they do, tell them how connected to them that makes you feel, see if you can help meet that need, and let them know you're not going anywhere.

Loving Your Partner Well

You can affirm your Two by offering a lot of physical affection and reminders of how precious they are to you, taking cues from how they show their love and reciprocating it. Twos need help remembering that they don't need to say yes to everything and that doing so will only take attention away from what is truly theirs to do. Remind your partner that they deserve their own love and care as much as anyone else does, and then help them prioritize it.

COMMUNICATION STYLE

Twos are verbal processors. It's essential for them to talk things out so they can think them through, and your attention to that fact will communicate that you care about them. They are intuitive and will pick up on your emotions and body language, so being open and honest will help them feel more connected to you. If your Two takes on a complaining tone in a conversation, that's probably a sign that they are having difficulty expressing a need. Help them bring it forward by gently expressing curiosity about what they want and encourage them to be more direct with you in the future, affirming your commitment to them no matter what their needs may be.

It's hard for a Two to not take criticism personally. Be aware that any negative feedback can feel as though you're saying "I don't like you," so make sure you reaffirm your love for them at the end of any difficult conversation.

NAVIGATING CONFLICT TOGETHER

Twos like to stay optimistic, which is difficult when relational struggles occur. They have a very strong side, too, which can make an appearance in times of conflict. When a Two gets angry or especially emotional, it often means that they have an unmet need or have neglected their own needs for too long and need to take some time for themselves. Let their emotion remind you to move in and offer love and support. They may not know how to talk about what they need, so your ability to ask them gentle questions and allow room for them to express themselves will go a long way in helping you restore harmony and connection.

IT'S NOT PERSONAL

Don't take it personally if your Type Two "over-cares" for you. Take the time to help them consider their motivations and attend to any feelings of their own they may be denying with their helping. Remember that they seek to be valuable in your eyes through what they do for you, so instead of letting this behavior push you away, use the opportunity to remind them of how lovable and worthy they are already—in God's eyes and in yours, too.

Practical Tips for Your Type Combination

Although there is no best combination of Enneagram types, using Enneagram wisdom will provide you with a new, shared language for navigating the struggles and triumphs of being together and specific ways to love each other well. Commit to learning about your own type, and then use the practice for your type combination to grow together. One way you can do this is by taking time to show your Two how loved and appreciated they are regardless of anything they do.

Helpful practices for every type in a relationship with a Two:

- *If you're a One:* Set aside time to focus solely on your partner.

- *If you're a Two:* Do self-care together and avoid giving too much of yourself away outside your own relationship.

- *If you're a Three:* Make time for rest; connection; and patient, attentive listening as you learn together how to attend to your emotions.

- *If you're a Four:* Help your partner engage their creativity and their feelings.

- *If you're a Five:* Be generous with your time and attention toward your partner.

- *If you're a Six:* Take time every day to share your thoughts, the happenings of the day, and to express any needs you might have together.

- *If you're a Seven:* Stay present with your partner in communication and conflict.

- *If you're an Eight:* Access your soft side. Being vulnerable with your partner will help them feel connected to you and offer an opportunity for them to be the strong one.

- *If you're a Nine:* Engage conflicts as they come up as a strategy for staying connected.

Indeed, nothing in all creation will ever be able to separate us from the love of God that is revealed in Christ Jesus our Lord.

—ROMANS 8:39, NLT

3

THE ACHIEVER

Understanding Your
Type Three Partner

Enneagram Threes inspire us every day with their ability to set and achieve goals, adapting to what others need them to be in any given situation. But did you know that part of what fuels a Three's fast pace is disconnection from their own feelings? It can be surprising to learn that, although they seem very self-assured, they actually need lots of encouragement from you, and as their partner you can play a huge role in reminding them that they don't have to be anything but themselves to be loved.

LIES THREES BELIEVE

It's important to recognize the false stories your Type Three partner believes so you can offer them the truth and compassion they need to let go of the narratives that keep them stuck and support them on their growth journey.

LIE #1: I must always be working toward my goals in order to be a success.

Threes get a lot of their identity from what they do, so it's important to give them praise and approval for the things they *are* apart from what they achieve. Fear of failure fuels their tendency to overwork, so help them rest when they need it.

LIE #2: The images I project of myself are more valuable than who I really am.

Type Threes can get lost in playing roles, shape-shifting their personalities into what they think people find admirable and forgetting who they are at their core. Help your partner remember that God created their authentic self, loved them before they ever did anything amazing, and will keep loving them even if they never do another awesome thing.

Loving Your Partner Well

Your Type Three partner will need you to help them prioritize relaxation and just *being* together. Often Threes will work to the point of exhaustion, so scheduling time to relax together is a good way to foster connection and intimacy, as is making space in your relationship for places where they don't feel compelled to achieve. Threes need to know that they make you happy, so verbalize your love, letting them know you're proud of them and why. Your affirmation is especially powerful when you catch your Three just being themselves and not performing in any way.

COMMUNICATION STYLE

Threes are generally good communicators, with a confident, solutions-oriented speaking style, and your partner appreciates you communicating in direct ways like they do. They truly appreciate honest feedback, but be gentle when offering criticism. Because they try so hard to be competent, it can feel really vulnerable to feel as though they failed you. Cultivating a safe space for them to share can really benefit your relationship, especially because talking about feelings is hard for them. It helps if you can lead the way, modeling being open about your feelings while not making them talk about feelings or the relationship for longer than necessary. When your partner does share, be present and encouraging, ask good questions, and tell them how much you appreciate their openness.

COMMUNICATION TIP

Threes truly want to meet their partner's needs, but they may struggle with knowing how to do that. Providing them with detailed information about what makes you feel loved will ensure you're both happy in the long run.

NAVIGATING CONFLICT TOGETHER

The ability to recognize your partner's underlying type-related struggles can help you be less reactive to them and more compassionate, even in times of conflict. Conflict can arise with Threes when they feel that their image is being threatened, that they're failing, that they're being criticized unjustly, or that they're being blamed or embarrassed. When feelings of conflict arise, your partner may quickly move into action or engage their critical thinking skills to get things sorted out, which can make them seem cold or unfeeling. You can help them move through this by encouraging them to slow down and communicate with you about how they are feeling and affirming that they are valuable and beloved regardless of their performance.

IT'S NOT PERSONAL

Don't take it personally if your Three is competitive with you. Remember they feel a strong need to be the best because they think their achievement is what makes them valuable. When you notice your partner in this pattern, share your feelings about how their competitiveness might be affecting you. Then remind them that they don't have to win them all to earn your love.

Practical Tips for Your Type Combination

Although there is no best combination of Enneagram types, using Enneagram wisdom will provide you with a new, shared language for navigating the struggles and triumphs of being together and specific ways to love each other well. Commit to learning about your own type, and then use the practice for your type combination to grow together. Your Type Three partner needs to know that you love them for who they are and not what they do. Find ways to show your admiration of them each day.

Helpful practices for every type in a relationship with a Three:

- *If you're a One:* Set goals together for rest, play, and processing your emotions.

- *If you're a Two:* Both of you need practice identifying and honoring your emotions, so set aside time each day to share how you're feeling.

- *If you're a Three:* Take breaks from productivity to foster emotional connection with your partner.

- *If You're a Four:* Schedule downtime together to talk and dream in ways that open up your hearts, recognizing it doesn't come naturally to them as it does to you.

- *If you're a Five:* Be available for your partner to talk through their thoughts and feelings at the end of each day, and share yours, too.

- *If you're a Six:* Stay optimistic and set goals that balance their drive for achievement with your need for caution.

- *If you're a Seven:* You have the ability to infuse fun into the life of your hardworking Three! Put a fun activity you both enjoy on the calendar today.

- *If you're an Eight:* Let loose and have fun together!
- *If you're a Nine:* Schedule relaxation dates together to help your Three recharge.

— ENCOURAGEMENT FOR YOUR PARTNER —

See how very much our Father loves us, for He calls us His children, and that is what we are!

—1 JOHN 3:1, NLT

4

THE INDIVIDUALIST

Understanding Your
Type Four Partner

Enneagram Fours are the least ordinary people you know, but they don't believe that about themselves. Others experience them as sensitive, emotional, and highly self-aware people who often exude creativity. But did you know they have always felt as if they lack something essential within themselves that everyone else seems to have? Or that they're afraid that they will never truly belong anywhere? The growth journey of a Four is to finally embrace that they are loved and completely whole, just as they are.

LIES FOURS BELIEVE

We all have beliefs about who we are and how the world works, but often those beliefs are not true. Supporting your Type Four partner with the truth about who they really are can help them grow.

LIE #1: No one understands me.

Although Fours can tend to build an identity upon the fact that they could never be understood by anyone else, understanding is also the thing they long for most. You have a unique position as their partner to show them you *want* to understand their deepest and most precious parts and to remind them that God already does.

LIE #2: No one wants to "go deep" with me.

Fours like to delve into deeper topics of conversation quickly and are frankly bored and frustrated when others want to stay more surface level. They need to be reminded that their depth is a gift, even when other people can't access it as easily. Exploring deep subjects together as a couple will bond you in wonderful ways.

Loving Your Partner Well

Enneagram Fours feel most loved when their partner sets aside unhurried time for them. They have a genuine need to feel heard and long to be understood, so your attentiveness really helps them feel valued and cherished. Fours are idealistic and tend to yearn for a life just outside their reach, and their emotions fluctuate wildly throughout every day, so being a steady presence yourself will ground them. Connecting on an intimate, emotional level through verbal and physical means will have an enormous impact on how loved and accepted they feel.

COMMUNICATION STYLE

Fours are long processors who think and feel deeply, and their communication is oriented toward possibility and marked by talk of their personal feelings and experiences. They enjoy deep conversations and are good listeners, but they may also withdraw sometimes if they feel as though the person they are talking to isn't "getting" them. If you notice this, lean in and ask them to verbalize what they are feeling. They will return the favor by helping you navigate your emotion, too, providing an empathetic ear without jumping to trying to solve your problem.

If your Four is suddenly silent, don't assume they are upset or disengaging from you. They may just be processing something you said or trying to find the right words. Asking them about it and allowing them time to process will help them feel supported and seen.

NAVIGATING CONFLICT TOGETHER

Fours need to express their feelings in an authentic way, displaying big emotions or choosing to withdraw in times of conflict, and this can create friction in relationships. It's good to allow them space, but Fours really appreciate their partners reaching out to them after some time has passed. It's also important to let your partner know you value their feelings, even if you don't agree with what the feeling is causing them to believe, and to remember that it's more important for you to listen than to fix their issues. Fours tend to take a lot of their identity from how they feel, so invalidating their feelings makes it seem as though you're invalidating who they are, which will drive them deeper into feeling misunderstood and abandoned and lead you further from resolution.

IT'S NOT PERSONAL

Don't take it personally if your Four doesn't think you understand. Remember, their inner experience is one of feeling misunderstood, and they have felt different and sensed that they don't belong all their lives. Learn to lean in and listen as they share, giving them your full attention. Simply showing that you truly *desire* to understand them goes a long way.

Practical Tips for Your
Type Combination

Although there is no best combination of Enneagram types, using Enneagram wisdom will provide you with a new, shared language for navigating the struggles and triumphs of being together and specific ways to love each other well. Commit to learning about your own type, and then use the practice for your type combination to grow together. Connect with your Four by communicating how special and unique they are to you and that you see them and desire to understand them, too.

Helpful practices for every type in a relationship with a Four:

- *If you're a One:* Listen without fixing. Learn from their emotional expression.

- *If you're a Two:* Alternate times of connectedness with times you are independent.

- *If you're a Three:* Communicate with transparency, let your emotions surface, and make time for each other.

- *If You're a Four:* Talk together about all the things in your life that make you feel grateful.

- *If you're a Five:* Be honest when you need space, and be willing to sacrifice that space when your partner needs more intimacy.

- *If you're a Six:* Try not to get defensive when they express their feelings; simply support them and help them feel seen.

- *If you're a Seven:* Be present with your partner, asking good questions and responding without trying to lighten their darker moods.

- *If you're an Eight:* Be patient when they are trying to express themselves, and try not to take things personally.

- *If you're a Nine:* Set aside time for talking through things you've each been processing.

—— ENCOURAGEMENT FOR YOUR PARTNER ——

You are altogether beautiful, my darling; in you there is no flaw.

—SONG OF SOLOMON 4:7, NIV

5
THE OBSERVER

Understanding Your
Type Five Partner

Fives are focused, curious learners who dive deep into the subjects that interest them, craving knowledge to help them figure everything out so they feel competent and secure in a world that can demand too much. It's helpful for the partners of Fives to realize that they feel as though they have to carefully ration their limited internal resources so they don't experience the devastation of being depleted. Your love and support mean so much. It's also good to remember that it costs them dearly to expend their energy and that it means they love you when they do.

LIES FIVES BELIEVE

Gaining greater understanding of the false narratives that rule your partner's thoughts can help you love and care for them in more targeted ways that are anchored in truth.

LIE #1: I need to have everything figured out, or I'm not safe.
It's impossible to know everything there is to know, so help your Five accept that some things will remain a mystery and that it's God who ultimately keeps them safe.

LIE #2: My thoughts are my best source of information.
It's undeniable that your partner has amazing mental capabilities, but they are missing out on the wisdom of their body and the data their emotions offer by staying only in their heads. Encouraging them to do more physical movement and pay more attention to emotion will support them in great ways.

Loving Your Partner Well

Your Five will benefit from your understanding of their desire to be self-sufficient and protective of their energy, even as you seek to help them realize that they have far more inner resources than they think they do. Being independent yourself, telling them how much you value their contributions, and keeping your Five's confidences will help them feel happy and secure in your relationship. Remind them often that you are there for them, that you long to support them when they need you, and that God will always provide every resource they could ever need in plentiful measure.

COMMUNICATION STYLE

Fives get a reputation for being introverted because in conversation, they tend to observe more than participate. This is more a matter of gathering information and collecting their thoughts than being shy, however. Because of this, they tend to be excellent, curious listeners who respect others by not pressing for personal information and prefer others to do the same. Fives can be quite talkative and engaged if the subject matter interests them, so you can often draw them more into conversation by asking them about their thoughts. Your genuine interest makes them feel very loved and valued. It costs Fives a lot to share, so they may leave a conversation abruptly if they feel depleted by the energy expenditure.

Don't spring things on your Five; rather, give them plenty of notice and information about what you want from them. This will help them feel more prepared, and it will help you get your needs met, too.

NAVIGATING CONFLICT TOGETHER

Knowing your partner's type-related patterns is important for many reasons, but it's vital when it comes to handling conflict. When a Five feels overwhelmed, intruded upon, or as though they're incompetent, they are more likely to get into conflict with others. They tend to detach from the situation and isolate themselves when this happens, preferring to process what's going on in their minds on their own. Many Fives even have a private "safe space" where they go to process. This can make their partners feel stressed, but it's important to give your Five the time and space they need and then invite them to express their thoughts and feelings when they feel ready to engage.

IT'S NOT PERSONAL

Don't take it personally if your Five needs some time away. Remember, your partner feels a strong need to conserve their energy, so they tend to withdraw from situations before they get depleted. Good communication and check-ins can help you stay in sync.

Practical Tips for Your Type Combination

Although there is no best combination of Enneagram types, using Enneagram wisdom will provide you with a new, shared language for navigating the struggles and triumphs of being together and specific ways to love each other well. Commit to learning about your own type, and then use the practice for your type combination to grow together. One way to love your Five well is by reassuring them that their needs are never a problem for you.

Helpful practices for every type in a relationship with a Five:

- *If you're a One:* Find ways to acknowledge your partner's competence, and be careful with being overly critical.

- *If you're a Two:* Connect through sharing your emotions, and don't fear their need for time away.

- *If you're a Three:* Take time away together, and respect your Five's energy level.

- *If you're a Four:* Honor their thinking, and show them how to engage with their emotions more.

- *If you're a Five:* Challenge each other to listen to your bodies and emotions every day.

- *If you're a Six:* Schedule time to enjoy your common interests.

- *If you're a Seven:* Find ways to be spontaneous together; encourage their participation in life.

- *If you're an Eight:* Help your Five take action on things that are important to them.

- *If you're a Nine:* Engage any conflict as it arises, and find ways to be physically active together.

And this same God who takes care of me will supply all your needs from his glorious riches, which have been given to us in Christ Jesus.

—PHILIPPIANS 4:19, NLT

6

THE LOYALIST

Understanding Your
Type Six Partner

Sixes are faithful, strong, and trustworthy, and in their presence others feel safe and supported. They are excellent troubleshooters, and they often see what the rest of us miss. But did you know that their mind can get stuck focusing on worst-case scenarios so they can prepare a plan in case everything goes wrong? Your Six needs you to acknowledge the possibility of the worst case, but they also need you to help balance it with everything that could go right, too. They need your assurance, support, and reminders that God is their ultimate source of security.

LIES SIXES BELIEVE

When you're aware of the lies your partner believes, you are better able to encourage them with what's true. Remember to be gentle and compassionate as you guide them toward new ways of thinking.

LIE #1: I always need to be on the lookout for problems and have a plan for when things go wrong.
Sixes are amazing troubleshooters, but being able to see every potential problem can mean it's hard *not* to see how everything could fall apart. Sixes need to be reminded that most things *will* work out and that although they can never avoid every potential problem, if problems do arise, they will have the courage to overcome them, and they will also have the support they need from those who care.

LIE #2: I'm not brave.
Sixes can vary in their response to fear. One type of Six will run toward what makes them afraid, another Six will freeze in the face of fear, and others are a combination of these responses depending on the situation. All Sixes are brave, as demonstrated each and every day when they feel their fears and act anyway. It's honestly pretty remarkable. Applaud your Six when they take action on matters that require their courage.

Loving Your Partner Well

The biggest gift you can give your Type Six partner is to help them build confidence and trust in who God created them to be. One way to do this is by affirming their decision-making ability and calling attention to all the good decisions they have made in the past. It's also good to allow your Six plenty of time to verbally process with you, as they tend to figure out what they think as they speak it aloud. Sixes need a lot of reassurance from their partners, so remind them that everything will be okay and let them know how much confidence you have in them.

COMMUNICATION STYLE

Sixes tend to be thoughtful and honest in their communication, and they tend to ask a lot of questions. Having good answers helps them feel secure and quiets the "inner committee" in their mind that is constantly peppering them with "what-ifs" and ways things could go wrong. This can make them seem suspicious or overly cautious, as can their tendency to poke holes in plans that don't seem safe to them. When they are relaxed and feel safe, however, Sixes can be some of the warmest, wittiest people you know. Sixes can benefit from a partner who listens well and recognizes their need for support when their anxiety is running the show.

COMMUNICATION TIP

Sixes need your reassurance, especially when you need to talk about heavier topics. Verbally communicating your commitment and love to them and demonstrating your emotional and physical faithfulness are important at any time, but especially in conversations that could bring up feelings of uncertainty.

NAVIGATING CONFLICT TOGETHER

Sixes can experience conflict in their relationships when they feel pressured or blamed or when their anxious thoughts shift into overdrive. It's important for you to remember that Sixes feel as though their reactions are rational and logical. Meeting them in their reaction and avoiding the temptation to tell them that their worries are unfounded will help your partner feel validated and heard. After you have acknowledged the problem, you can offer ideas for solving it and resolving the conflict together.

If your partner gets defensive, it may be a sign that you should take a break and come back to talk more later, after you each have processed a bit. Reassure your Six that reconciliation is your goal and that conflict doesn't change your commitment to them.

IT'S NOT PERSONAL

Don't take it personally if your Type Six partner questions you or double-checks your info—they double- and triple-check themselves, too. Remember that your partner has a strong desire to feel certain and prepared for what's coming next, and gathering information helps them feel safe, so be thoughtful and patient when answering their questions.

Practical Tips for Your Type Combination

Although there is no best combination of Enneagram types, using Enneagram wisdom will provide you with a new, shared language for navigating the struggles and triumphs of being together and specific ways to love each other well. Commit to learning about your own type and then use the practice for your type combination to grow together. Your Type Six needs to know that they are safe and secure. As their partner, you can help them feel secure in your relationship by using some of the following practices.

Helpful practices for every type in a relationship with a Six:

- *If you're a One:* Find ways to have fun and be spontaneous together.

- *If you're a Two:* Reassure your partner when they worry; show your appreciation of them.

- *If you're a Three:* Spend time listening to your partner and helping them set goals for the future.

- *If you're a Four:* Take your partner's concerns seriously, and offer plenty of reassurance when they need it.

- *If you're a Five:* Remind your Six how much you trust them as a way to help them learn to trust in themselves. Take time together to explore subjects that interest you both.

- *If you're a Six:* Bolster each other's confidence and self-trust as often as you can.

- *If you're a Seven:* Validate your Six's worries, and then help them see how things could turn out okay.

- *If you're an Eight:* Share how appreciative you are for the ways your Six looks out for you.

- *If you're a Nine:* Keep talking, even in conflict, and make sure your partner knows how much you trust them.

—— ENCOURAGEMENT FOR YOUR PARTNER ——

How precious is Your unfailing love, O God! All humanity finds shelter in the shadow of Your wings.

—PSALM 36:5–7, NLT

7

THE ENTHUSIAST

Understanding Your
Type Seven Partner

Enneagram Sevens have a reputation for always being lighthearted, creative, and optimistic, always on the hunt for the next adventure and making plans for future fun. But did you know that your Seven's fast pace is part of an effort to avoid all pain and boredom? Or that they are secretly afraid of any limitations impeding the satisfaction they seek? As their partner, you can support your Seven's dreams while encouraging them to live with more balance and the confidence that God will never let them miss out on anything that's meant for them.

LIES SEVENS BELIEVE

Your awareness of the false narratives your partner believes will help you support and care for them in ways that affirm what's really true.

LIE #1: Dark feelings are a bummer—and no one wants that part of me anyway.
Enneagram Sevens prefer to focus on the positive, so it's no wonder that they shy away from sadness and pain. Reassure your Seven that all the shades of their feelings, dark and light, are welcomed and accepted and that embracing all their feelings will give them the fullest experience of their own life.

LIE #2: My fulfillment exists somewhere in the future.
Sevens can tend to believe that if they slow down, their troubles might catch them, so they prefer to look to the future for their hope of better things. Help your partner ground into the present moment by calling attention to all the wonderful things that God has provided right here, in this moment.

Loving Your Partner Well

Your Seven will appreciate efforts you make toward keeping life fun and interesting. Get excited about their many ideas and join them in working to make them a reality. When they take on too much, help them not slip into self-criticism, as Sevens can be quite hard on themselves. Instead, help them decide which things really matter to them and help direct their focus there. Affirm to them that, as their partner, you are committed to helping meet their needs and achieve their dreams, and remind them that God will never let them miss out on what is truly meant for them.

COMMUNICATION STYLE

Sevens have an energetic talking style, full of gesticulation, ideas, and stories with twists, turns, and sequences that are entertaining but sometimes confusing for others to follow. Their communication is a good window into how busy their minds truly are. They tend to cover a lot of subjects in one conversation, and their speech is full of creative ideas and possibilities. If a difficult subject arises, however, Sevens will want to change the subject or at least "reframe" it into something positive by making a joke or finding a silver lining. Help them practice staying with hard subjects a bit longer by asking them how they feel about it each time you notice this happening, and when they share, let them know that you're glad they shared that part of themselves with you.

COMMUNICATION TIP

Your Seven wants your undivided attention when they are talking to you, even if that's hard for them to give you when you are talking. Model this for them as they tell you their many stories, and you'll make them feel loved and valued.

NAVIGATING CONFLICT TOGETHER

Sevens can get into conflict with others when they overcommit and aren't able to keep their promises, making others feel forgotten and unimportant. Others may criticize them for being unreliable, which will make them feel defensive and self-critical. Support your partner by helping them be realistic about what they can accomplish in a day, and be compassionate but honest with them regarding how their tendency to juggle too much can actually limit them and the positive impact they truly desire to have. After working through conflict, it's often helpful to lighten the mood and share how appreciative you are to have a partner that cares so much about your relationship. A celebration might even be in order! It takes real work for a Seven to do uncomfortable things, so rewarding them for staying in the discomfort can help them be willing to do it the next time it happens, too.

IT'S NOT PERSONAL

Don't take it personally if your Type Seven interrupts you, either with words or with their body language (think enthusiastic nodding). Chances are, they're just excited about what you're saying and can't stop themselves from showing you how much they are connecting with what you're talking about. Communicating to your partner about how you feel when you get interrupted and encouraging them to make adjustments to their approach may help avoid the offense altogether.

Practical Tips for Your Type Combination

Although there is no best combination of Enneagram types, using Enneagram wisdom will provide you with a new, shared language for navigating the struggles and triumphs of being together, and specific ways to love each other well. Commit to learning about your own type and then use the practice for your type combination to grow together. Your Seven needs to know you will take care of them, and have fun with them, too.

Helpful practices for every type in a relationship with a Seven:

- *If you're a One:* Be careful with criticism. Plan adventures together.

- *If you're a Two:* Help your Seven explore their emotional world and grow in compassion for others.

- *If you're a Three:* Keep connection strong by scheduling fun, and keep each other accountable for feeling your feelings.

- *If you're a Four:* Be playful, and join them in their plans, whether or not you think they are a good idea.

- *If you're a Five:* Learn about something new together.

- *If you're a Six:* Collaborate with your partner, and resist poking holes in their big ideas.

- *If you're a Seven:* Help each other keep your expectations realistic. Enjoy each other's energy.

- *If you're an Eight:* Be excited about your partner's ideas, and help make them happen.

- *If you're a Nine:* Let your Seven energize you as you help them make solid, concrete plans for executing their big ideas.

—— ENCOURAGEMENT FOR YOUR PARTNER ——

The LORD will always guide you; He will satisfy you in a sun-scorched land and strengthen your frame. You will be like a well-watered garden, like a spring whose waters never fail.

—ISAIAH 58:11, NIV

8

THE PROTECTOR

Understanding Your Type Eight Partner

If you are loved by an Eight, you know it. Eights are passionate and committed partners who will gladly give you their unwavering loyalty and protection, putting themselves in harm's way to ensure your safety. But did you know that beneath this tough exterior, there is the most tender, playful, loving, and caring of hearts? Or that they often feel very misunderstood by others? Despite their powerful presence, your Eight needs lots of love and proof of your commitment to them. As their partner, you can help them power down their protective stance by being a source of strength for them, too.

LIES EIGHTS BELIEVE

Understanding the false stories your partner believes can help you compassionately support them with the truth and help them grow past the limiting beliefs of their type.

LIE #1: **I'm too much.**

Eights have a lot of energy, so they frequently get this message from the world, and they internalize it. You can help by being a safe place for them to be their full selves. When Eights mature, they can develop more sensitivity and discernment about which situations can handle their full impact and which can't.

LIE #2: **I can't trust anyone as much as I trust myself; no one else will show up like I do.**

Eights do everything they can to avoid being weak and dependent, even if that means they shoulder all the burden, which is often easier for them than trusting that anyone will be there for them. Your consistency in being there for them will help them uproot this lie.

Loving Your Partner Well

More than anything else, an Eight needs someone who respects and appreciates their strength and helps them learn to value and reframe their own tenderness and sensitivity as a great source of that strength. Remind your partner that they were not meant to carry the weight of the world; God is our ultimate source of trustworthy protection, and as their partner, you have their back, too. It's also really important that you encourage your hardworking Eight to make time for rest and physical forms of play. Self-care is hard for them to prioritize, but they need it.

COMMUNICATION STYLE

Type Eights are known for their direct, no-BS approach to communication. When something matters to them, they will speak passionately (even loudly) about the subject and project a sense that they alone have the truth about the subject. This intensity can be misunderstood as anger or hostility when they are really only demonstrating their commitment to truth and justice. They have zero hesitation about having hard conversations, and they can't stand it when others are dishonest or inauthentic. Eights are either all in or all out, and you will never be unsure about how they feel about something.

Eights have easy access to their anger (which is usually covering up more vulnerable feelings), but anger is often an Eight's passion bubbling to the surface. Try to avoid assuming they are mad at you and lean in to see if you can discover what's really going on.

NAVIGATING CONFLICT TOGETHER

Eights are not afraid of conflict. In fact, the intensity that conflict can bring can feel connective to them, as if the two of you are sharing an energy-charged moment. It has been said that Eights like to have something to "push against" because it makes them feel alive and vital. This means your Eight won't be shy about sharing controversial or contrary opinions, just to see if anyone is in the mood for a good ol' argument, and they don't mind you differing in opinion, as long as they feel that you hear and respect theirs, too. Being aware that conflict doesn't necessarily mean that your Eight is mad at you can help you engage in a healthier way.

IT'S NOT PERSONAL

Don't take it personally if your Eight struggles to trust you. Remember, they're very fearful about being betrayed and think they always need to be on guard. Being consistent in your trustworthiness and allowing your Eight time off from being "the strong one" can go a long way in helping them trust you more.

Practical Tips for Your Type Combination

Although there is no best combination of Enneagram types, using Enneagram wisdom will provide you with a new, shared language for navigating the struggles and triumphs of being together and specific ways to love each other well. Commit to learning about your own type and then use the practice for your type combination to grow together. One way to love your Type Eight partner well is by reassuring them that you've got their back and will never betray them.

Helpful practices for every type in a relationship with an Eight:

- *If you're a One:* Your trustworthiness is a gift. Lean on each other and take turns leading.

- *If you're a Two:* Be honest and gentle with your Eight, and plan self-care dates.

- *If you're a Three:* Take time off from work to play and mess around.

- *If you're a Four:* Leave some emotional space for your partner to fill, and be strong for them sometimes, too.

- *If you're a Five:* Model healthy ways to withdraw for self-support and energy recharging.

- *If you're a Six:* Be decisive and take the lead when your Eight needs you to.

- *If you're a Seven:* Practice welcoming your tender feelings, and then reward yourself with fun.

- *If you're an Eight:* Take time to appreciate how you support each other.

- *If you're a Nine:* Speak up and hold your own to experience more connection.

Trust in the Lord with all your heart and lean not on your own understanding; in all your ways submit to him, and he will make your paths straight.

—PROVERBS 3:5–6, NIV

9

THE PEACEMAKER

Understanding Your Type Nine Partner

Enneagram Nines tend to be easygoing, adaptable, and laid-back. They're good listeners, and people love them because of how open-minded and accepting they can be. But did you know that much of this behavior is because Nines fear conflict? And that they may defer to someone else's opinion on something because they don't know what they really want? Your job as a partner is to help your Nine wake up to their feelings, take action in the direction of their passions, and make the impact on the world that God designed them for.

LIES NINES BELIEVE

Knowing the narratives that your partner believes about themselves can help you understand and support them in just the ways they need it, affirming what's true so they can grow past their type's limitations.

LIE #1: **My life is better if I avoid all conflict.**
Because Nines like to be comfortable, it makes sense why they would want to avoid conflict. But there's no such thing as a life without conflict, so learning to navigate it well when it arises between the two of you will help your Nine strengthen their connection to what matters to them and help you both get the life you really want.

LIE #2: **My voice doesn't matter as much as other people's do.**
Enneagram Nines often prefer to put others before themselves because they feel that asserting their own desires will cause disharmony in their relationships. As a result, Nines tend to be asleep to their own value as an individual. Help your partner realize that their voice matters, because *they* matter, to others and to God. You can help your partner realize that they matter by validating their opinions, seeking their insight, and applauding their efforts to speak up.

Loving Your Partner Well

Nines can tend to "merge" with what others want instead of expressing their own desires, so it helps if you can encourage your Nine to express their own opinions and then let them know you're glad they did. Try not to talk over your partner, and always validate what they say, giving them space to talk even if it takes a while for them to get to their point. Your support and love will help your partner wake up to the truth that God has created them to make an important impact on the world.

COMMUNICATION STYLE

People love talking to Nines because they are so amiable and accepting of all kinds of people and they truly value others' perspectives. They are encouraging, thoughtful listeners, and they really care about people, which shows in their conversational style. They don't seem as though they have many opinions, so it can be easy for others to just assume they don't. This is because it's hard for them to communicate what they need; it helps if others show genuine interest in what they are sharing so they feel more able to open up. Try not to rush them as they are talking, thank them for sharing, and do whatever you can to show how much you value what they've contributed.

COMMUNICATION TIP

It's helpful if you ask your Nine what their thoughts or feelings are about something before you share yours. This sends the message that you value their input and decreases the likelihood that they'll agree to something they didn't actually want.

NAVIGATING CONFLICT TOGETHER

Nines do everything they can to avoid getting into conflict because they don't want to risk losing connection with you or other important people in their lives. But some conflict is necessary, and you can't have a healthy, connected relationship without it. Knowing your Nine's patterns can help you lean in and be compassionate, even in times of conflict. Watch for times when you see your partner "numbing out," and see if you can help them be curious about something they might be avoiding addressing. Be gentle and nonconfrontational, and give them lots of affirmation about the solidity of your relationship following any disagreements.

IT'S NOT PERSONAL

Don't take it personally if your Nine doesn't seem to be listening. They use a lot of energy in trying to maintain inner and outer harmony, so sometimes it's easier for them to give the appearance that they are listening (especially when it's an uncomfortable subject) when they really aren't. Being direct about the level of attention you need will help them stay focused on the conversation, as will asking their opinion from time to time.

Practical Tips for Your Type Combination

Although there is no best combination of Enneagram types, using Enneagram wisdom will provide you with a new, shared language for navigating the struggles and triumphs of being together and specific ways to love each other well. Commit to learning about your own type and then use the practice for your type combination to grow together. Your Nine needs your help reclaiming their sense of self, awakening to their passions, and reconnecting to their worth as a person.

Helpful practices for every type in a relationship with a Nine:

- *If you're a One:* Work together on projects that matter to both of you.

- *If you're a Two:* Engage conflict as it arises, and give your partner alone time when they need it.

- *If you're a Three:* Help build your Nine's confidence by celebrating their successes.

- *If you're a Four:* Be present with each other, and don't let too much go unsaid.

- *If you're a Five:* Make dates to do physical activities together. This will help you connect and unwind your minds.

- *If you're a Six:* Spend time talking about your individual hopes and dreams; then make plans to achieve them.

- *If you're a Seven:* Ask about your partner's dreams, and help them make plans to achieve them.

- *If you're an Eight:* Encourage your Nine to be assertive and strong, even with you.

- *If you're a Nine:* Practice talking about all subjects together, even the hard ones.

— ENCOURAGEMENT FOR YOUR PARTNER —

And the very hairs on your head are all numbered. So don't be afraid; you are more valuable to God than a whole flock of sparrows.

—LUKE 12:7, NLT

CLOSING

Proverbs 20:5 reminds us "the purposes of a person's heart are deep waters," so to plumb a heart's depths requires a deep system. The Enneagram is one of the best resources I have found to help guide us into those deep places and show us how to embody all that God has placed lovingly into our hearts and minds. It offers us a guide we can use to grow past the limiting behaviors of our personalities, trusting that God will provide and perfect the offering of our authentic selves and inspire us to love with the compassion and grace our world needs so desperately.

This book is just an introduction, and you deserve to venture, in your personal journey, past what you have learned here. Promise me you will keep going. There is so much more to discover in yourself and in those you want to love well.

RESOURCES AND REFERENCES

I'm so thankful for all the resources that exist today, on this list and elsewhere, for those who wish to grow with the help of the Enneagram. In addition to the sources listed here, so many gifted coaches and teachers have impacted my knowledge of this incredibly complicated system. I'm truly grateful.

BOOKS

Chestnut, Beatrice. *The Complete Enneagram: 27 Paths to Greater Self-Knowledge*. Berkeley, CA: She Writes Press, 2013.

Cron, Ian Morgan, and Suzanne Stabile. *The Road Back to You: An Enneagram Journey to Self-Discovery*. Downers Grove, IL: IVP Books, 2016.

Daniels, David N., and Virginia Price. *The Essential Enneagram: The Definitive Personality Test and Self-Discovery Guide*. San Francisco: Harper San Francisco, 2000.

McCord, Beth and Jeff. *Becoming Us: Using the Enneagram to Create a Thriving Gospel-Centered Marriage*. Nashville, TN: Morgan James Publishing, 2020.

Riso, Don Richard, and Russ Hudson. *The Wisdom of the Enneagram: The Complete Guide to Psychological and Spiritual Growth for the Nine Personality Types*. New York: Bantam, 1999.

Stabile, Suzanne. *The Path Between Us: An Enneagram Journey to Healthy Relationships*. Downers Grove, IL: IVP Books, 2018.

Vancil, Marilyn. *Self to Lose—Self to Find: A Biblical Approach to the 9 Enneagram Types*. Enumclaw, WA: Redemption Press, 2016.

WEBSITES

The Enneagram in Business: TheEnneagraminBusiness.com

The Enneagram Institute: EnneagramInstitute.com

INDEX

A

Achievers. *See* Threes

C

Center of intelligence, 5
Chestnut, Beatrice, 7
The Complete Enneagram (Chestnut), 7
Core desires, 18
Core fears, 18
Core weaknesses, 18
2 Corinthians
  9:8, 63
  12:9–10, 86–87

D

Deuteronomy
  31:6, 70

E

Eights
  Bible passage, 87
  communication style, 81, 82
  conflicts, 82
  core motivations, 21
  growth, 87
  interacting with others, 81
  as partners, 141–143
  reflecting God, 86
  in relationships with, 143–145
  in security, 82–83

self-assessment, 16
in stress, 82–83
subtypes, 84–85
wings, 84
Enneagram
  center of intelligence, 5
  and faith, 2
  history of, 2
  instincts, 7
  and relationships, 3–5
  security numbers, 5–6
  stress numbers, 5
  subtypes, 7
  wings, 8
Enthusiasts. *See* Sevens
Ephesians
  1:17, 62
  2:10, 94
  4:2, 39

F

Fives
  Bible passage, 63
  communication style, 57, 58
  conflicts, 58
  core motivations, 20
  growth, 63
  interacting with others, 57
  as partners, 123–125
  reflecting God, 61–62
  in relationships with, 125–127
  in security, 58–59

self-assessment, 13
in stress, 58–59
subtypes, 61
wings, 59–60
Fours
Bible passage, 55
communication style, 49–50
conflicts, 50
core motivations, 19
growth, 55
interacting with others, 49
as partners, 117–119
reflecting God, 54
in relationships with, 120–121
in security, 50–51
self-assessment, 12
in stress, 50–51
subtypes, 52–53
wings, 52

G

Genesis
1:31A, 31

H

Healing messages, 18
Helpers. *See* Twos

I

Individualists. *See* Fours
Instincts, 7
Isaiah
43:4–28, 55
58:11, 139

J

Jeremiah
9:24, 87
29:11, 71
John
13:34, 97
14:27, 95

1 John
3:1, 115
4:16, 39

L

Lamentations
3:10, 2
Loyalists. *See* Sixes
Luke
12:7, 151

M

Mark
1:11, 47
8:34–36, 1
Matthew
11:28–30, 31

N

Nines
Bible passage, 95
communication style, 89, 90
conflicts, 90
core motivations, 21
growth, 95
interacting with others, 89
as partners, 147–149
reflecting God, 94
in relationships with, 150–151
in security, 90–91
self-assessment, 16
in stress, 90–91
subtypes, 92–93
wings, 92

O

Observers. *See* Fives
Ones
Bible passage, 31
communication style, 25, 26
conflicts, 26

Ones (*continued*)
 core motivations, 18
 growth, 31
 interacting with others, 25
 as partners, 99–101
 reflecting God, 30
 in relationships with, 102–103
 in security, 26–28
 self-assessment, 9
 in stress, 26–28
 subtypes, 28–29
 wings, 28
One-to-one instinct, 7

P

Peacemakers. *See* Nines
Perfectionists. *See* Ones
1 Peter
 4:10, 21
Philippians
 1:9–11, 23
 4:19, 127
Protectors. *See* Eights
Proverbs
 3:5–6, 145
 20:5, 153
Psalms
 16:11, 79
 23:1–2, 47
 26:6, 103
 36:5–7, 133
 107:9, 79
 139:14, 55
Pythagoras, 2

R

Relationships, Enneagram and, 3–5
Romans
 8:39, 109

S

Security numbers, 6
Self-preservation instinct (SP), 7
Sevens
 Bible passage, 79
 communication style, 73, 74
 conflicts, 74
 core motivations, 20–21
 growth, 79
 interacting with others, 73
 as partners, 135–138
 reflecting God, 78–79
 in relationships with, 138–139
 in security, 74–75
 self-assessment, 15
 in stress, 74–75
 subtypes, 76–77
 wings, 76
Sexual instinct (SX), 7
Sixes
 Bible passage, 71
 communication style, 65–66
 conflicts, 66
 core motivations, 20
 growth, 71
 interacting with others, 65
 as partners, 129–131
 reflecting God, 69–70
 in relationships with, 132–133
 in security, 66–67
 self-assessment, 14
 in stress, 66–67
 subtypes, 68–69
 wings, 68
Social instinct (SO), 7
Song of Solomon
 4:7, 121
Stress numbers, 6
Subtypes, 7

T

Threes
Bible passage, 47
communication style, 41–42
conflicts, 42
core motivations, 19
growth, 47
interacting with others, 41
as partners, 111–113
reflecting God, 46
in relationships with, 114–115
in security, 42–43
self-assessment, 11
in stress, 42–43
subtypes, 44–45
wings, 44
Twos
Bible passage, 39

communication style, 33–34
conflicts, 34
core motivations, 18–19
growth, 39
interacting with others, 33
as partners, 105–107
reflecting God, 38
in relationships with, 107–109
in security, 34–35
self-assessment, 10
in stress, 34–35
subtypes, 36–37
wings, 36

W

Wings, 8

Acknowledgments

Over the years, people have told me, "You should write a book!" but until that afternoon in July when Rockridge Press reached out to me, I wondered if I'd ever make that a reality. I'm incredibly grateful for this opportunity to help couples grow closer using the tool of the Enneagram, as my husband and I have.

The work of so many has provided the foundation for all I've written here. My teachers, mentors, colleagues, clients, friends, and family have been instrumental in teaching me what is written in these pages. I thank God for your presence in my life.

Special thanks to Beth McCord, Jim Gum, Suzanne Stabile, Father Richard Rohr, Russ Hudson, Don Riso, Chris Heuertz, Kristi Rowles, Steph Barron Hall, Vanessa Fernandez, Alison Speerbrecker, Nancy Bartelt, Bethanee Riddle, Terrissa Chavers, and Emily Schloerb.

Finally, I'd like to thank my family for their encouragement, support, and unwavering belief in me. To my kids, Eli, Willow, and Silas: You are all such treasures to me and probably the best teachers I'll ever have. I love you forever, and I'm so proud to be your mom!

To my husband: Shane, you're my best thing. Thank you for reminding me that I'm beloved, day after day after day. I love you more than words can express.

About the Author

Dani Cooper is a certified Enneagram teacher and coach for individuals, couples, and teams. She and her husband of 25 years live rurally outside Kansas City with their three kids. She finds great joy in guiding others into the deep waters of their own hearts and helping them discover who they've been lovingly created to be. Connect with her at DeepWatersEnneagram.com or on Instagram @DeepWatersEnneagram.